Voices *as one*

Contemporary Hymnal

Vocal Edition, 6591

WORLD LIBRARY PUBLICATIONS
a division of J. S. Paluch Co., Inc.
3825 North Willow Road
Schiller Park, Illinois 60176

Voices As One

WLP 6591
Second Printing

Also available:

Keyboard accompaniment	WLP 6590
Guitar accompaniment	WLP 6597
CD	WLP 6594
Casssette	WLP 6592

ISBN 0-937690-67-8

WORLD LIBRARY PUBLICATIONS
a division of J. S. Paluch Company, Inc.
3825 North Willow Road, Schiller Park, IL 60176
phone: 1 800 566-6150
fax: 1 888 WLP-FAX1
e-mail: wlpcs@jspaluch.com
www.wlp.jspaluch.com

Voices As One. What does that mean?

Are we referring to the faithful gathered in a worship space adorned with gold, stained glass, and beautiful garments, singing God's praises while a 200-voice choir sings out thick harmonies, and a huge pipe organ or praise band rocks the rafters with massive sound?

Or are we referring to the average community gathering each Sunday in a building which speaks of history, not wealth, raising their voices accompanied by the efforts of volunteer musicians?

Voices As One. It is both. And more!

Voices As One means the voice which speaks to the person on the street corner wearing filthy clothes, begging for food, and receiving a gift from a loving hand; the husband and wife having trouble in their marriage and finding comfort in the voice of a caring pastor and supportive neighbors; the teen who just can't relate to his or her parents and finds a youth minister to listen to the pain of lonely days; the voices of prisoners, addicts to drugs and alcohol, those who are abused, the list goes on. This is their hymnal; this is their voice.

Voices As One means the voices of those who have more than enough to eat and so share generously; those whose marriages are filled with love and give witness to those getting ready to marry; teens whose lives are filled with the joy of solid families and friends, who reach out to those who are lonely and hurting; those who are dedicated to living life to its fullest, sharing their happiness with all those around them.

This is their hymnal; this is their voice, too.

It's for someone doing great in school or struggling in school; for any-body with high or low self-esteem; those who are always happy or the one suffering depression. This is their hymnal, their voice.

These songs are about life, about the rituals of life, about God among us. The words and melodies in these pages are all about the journey that each of us makes. Many of the songs refer to passages of scripture while others are the result of lyrics inspired through prayer, meditation, and worship. These are songs that have touched many hearts and many lives—hearts and lives just like your own. Lives are transformed when we allow God to work in us and through us—through prayer, song, and all kinds of worship.

This collection is a resource for the community of faithful, and for your own faith journey. This book is called a "contemporary hymnal," but we believe it is also for those who are beyond their teen years, who are young at heart and filled with seasoned wisdom. We believe that people of all ages minister together and form some of the strongest communities by this bond of journeying with fresh eyes and wise perspectives.

Recall all the different people described at the beginning of this preface. Remember that we are all indeed one body in Christ—no one is excluded. As we foster our faith, we foster the faith of others as well. As we share in song, we make our lives a stronger song for others.

Since you're reading this preface you either were led to pick up a copy of Voices As One, or maybe someone—your youth minister, music minister, pastor, friend or family member—handed it to you. Whichever the case, you are part of the voice, the Church. You have been handed a companion for your journey, use it, share it as love handed down.

Voices As One is all voices, all people. No matter who you are, where you've been, or where the Spirit is leading you, you are part of this family of God.

All Will Be Well

REFRAIN

Cantor/All

All will be well, and all will be well, all

1.–5.   To Verses

man - ner of things will be well.

Final

well,   will be well,   will be well.

VERSES 1, 3, 5

Cantor

1. Our Lord___ said that all would be well, all
3. In all the doubts that shroud sim - ple truths, we
5. Our faith is firm and stands on the Word, the

To Refrain

1. man - ner of things would be well.___
3. pray for the wis - dom of God.___
5. Word that en - dures for all time.___

VERSES 2, 4, 6

Cantor

2. With all the sad - ness wrought in this world,___ the
4. Give us the faith to trust in your love,___ when
6. And so we pray to trust in the hope that all

To Refrain

2. good shall___ al - ways pre - vail.___
4. things are con- cealed from our view.___
6. man - ner of things shall be well.___

The Revelations of Divine Love, Chapter 32
Julian of Norwich
Adapt. by S.C.W.

Steven C. Warner
Text and music © 1993, WLP

2 Alleluia! Your Word, O Lord

Al - le - lu - ia!___ Al - le - lu - ia!___

Al - le - lu - ia!___ Al - le - lu - ia!___

Your_ Word, O Lord, is a light to us!

Al - le - lu - ia! May your

Word, O Lord, be a light to us!

Al - le - lu - ia!_____

Ed Bolduc
Text and music © 1998, WLP

3 Answer When I Call

REFRAIN

Repeat first time only

O God, an - swer when I call._____

VERSES

1. How long will we be dull of heart?___
2. O Lord, let the light of your coun - te - nance
3. For you a - lone are the Lord!___

1. Why do we love what is vain? The Lord does won - ders for
2. shine_ up - on___ us. _ You will hear_ me
3. You_ a - lone bring me peace. _ Guide me safe - ly

1. all who call up - on_____ him._____
2. in my time of dark - ness._____
3. home to rest in your em - brace._____

FINAL REFRAIN

O God, an - swer when I call._____

O God, an - swer when I call, O God.

Paul A. Tate
Text and music © 1998, WLP

Answer Me 4

REFRAIN

An-swer___ me._____ An-swer___ me._____

An - swer___ me._____ O_____ Lord.

1. I have been a stranger to my neighbor
   and an alien to my mother's children.
   The love I feel for you, O Lord, consumes me.
   I cannot forget those who fall upon me.
   Hear me, O Lord, you are my God.

2. I will pray to you, O Lord, for favor.
   You will answer me. Holy is your kindness.
   Answer me, O Lord, and find me worthy,
   you are my Lord. Endless is your mercy.
   Hear me, O Lord, you are my God.

3. See, the Lord listens to his children,
   and will not look down on his captive people.
   Heav'n and earth should praise the Lord, so worthy,
   who will save our world. Happy are those who praise him.
   Hear me, O Lord, you are my God.

Ed Bolduc
Text and music © 1993, WLP

5 At the Name of Jesus

VERSES

1. At the name of Je - sus ev - 'ry knee shall bow,
2. With your hearts en - throne him; there let him sub - due

1. ev - 'ry tongue con - fess him Lord, King of glo - ry
2. all that is not ho - ly, all that is not

1. now, King of glo - ry now.
2. true, all that is not true.

1. It is the Fa - ther's pleas - ure we should call him
2. — Chris - tians, this Lord Je - sus dwells with us a -

1. Lord, who from the be - gin - ning was the
2. gain, in his Fa - ther's wis - dom o'er the

1. might - y Word, was the might - y Word.
2. earth to reign, o'er the earth to reign.

REFRAIN

O— God, we a-dore— you.— O—

God, we bow—— down.— We ex - alt and— we

praise you,— led by your Spir - it_____ O

Ho - ly One, O Ho - ly One.

Vss.: Caroline Maria Noel, 1817–1877, alt.

Ed Bolduc
Text (ref.) and music © 1998, WLP

At the Table of the World 6

1. At the ta-ble of the world, some have plen-ty, some have none.
2. At the ta-ble of the world, some have hon-or, some have scorn.
3. Set the ta-ble of our God in the Church and in the world,

1. At the ta-ble of our God, all are plen-ti-ful-ly fed.
2. At the ta-ble of our God, all are wel-comed and ac-claimed.
3. Till the chil-dren, fed and loved, taste and see that life is good.

Blow a-mong us, Spir-it of God,_____ fill us with your

cour-age and care!_____ Hur-ri-cane and Breath,

2

take us on a jour-ney of love!_____

Brian Wren
Text © 1989, Hope Publishing Co.

Carl Johengen
Music © 1993, WLP

7 Awesome God

1. When he rolls up his sleeves, he ain't just "putting on the ritz."
Our God is an awesome God!
There's thunder in his footsteps and lightning in his fists.
Our God is an awesome God!

And the Lord he wasn't joking when he kicked 'em out of Eden.
It wasn't for no reason that he shed his blood.
His return is very close, and so you better be believing that
our God is an awesome God!

REFRAIN

Our God is an awe-some God! He__ reigns from__ heav-en a - bove with__ wis - dom,__ pow'r and love— Our__ God is an awe - some God! Our God! Our God is an awe - some God! Our God is an awe - some God!

2. And when the sky was starless in the void of the night,
Our God is an awesome God!
He spoke into the darkness and created the light.
Our God is an awesome God!

And judgment and wrath he poured out on Sodom,
the mercy and grace he gave us at the cross.
I hope that we have not too quickly forgotten that
our God is an awesome God!

Rich Mullins
Text and music © 1988, BMG Songs, Inc. (ASCAP)

Be Holy 8

REFRAIN

"Be ho - ly, be ho - ly,_____ for I, the Lord, your God, am ho - ly. Be ho - ly, be ho - ly_____ for I, the Lord, your God, am ho - ly."

(⌢) Last time

VERSES

1. O Lord, who will reach your heart?_____ "Those who
   Lord, who is in your heart?_____ "Those who
2. O Lord, who__ lives with-in__ you?__ "Those who
   Lord, who__ dwells with-in__ you?__ "Those who

1. walk blame-less - ly and__ are just to - ward all." O__
   speak on - ly truth and__ will slan - der__ no__ one." Re -
2. turn from all e - vil__ and hon - or__ the Lord." O__
   seek not__ their wel - fare__ but live for__ the Lord." Re -

To Refrain

1.-2. joice! Re - joice!__ They shall not__ be moved.

Be Still for the Presence of the Lord

1. Be still, for the pres-ence of the Lord, the
2. Be still, for the glo - ry of the Lord is
3. Be still, for the pow - er of the Lord is

1. Ho - ly One, is___ here. Come bow be -
2. shin - ing all a - round. He burns with
3. mov - ing in this__ place. He comes to___

1. fore him now with rev - er - ence and__ fear.
2. ho - ly fire, with splen - dor he is__ crowned.
3. cleanse and heal, to min - is - ter his__ grace.

1. In him no sin is found, we stand on
2. How awe-some is the sight, our ra - diant
3. No work too hard for him, in faith re -

1. ho - ly ground. Be still, for the pres-ence of the
2. King of light. Be still, for the glo - ry of the
3. ceive from him. Be still, for the pow - er of the

1. Lord, the Ho - ly One, is here.
2. Lord is shin - ing all a - round.
3. Lord is mov - ing in this place.

David J. Evans
Text and music © 1986, Kingsway's Thankyou Music

1. Come, Lord, into our souls, your words will make us whole;
   heal the broken-hearted ones.
   In the darkness, be our light, be the stronghold of our life;
   Listen to our plea, O Lord! Stay with us! Be present, Lord!

REFRAIN

Be with me, Lord,—— when I'm in trou-ble.
Be with me, Lord,—— when I'm in need.——
Out of the—— depths—— I'm cry-ing to you,——
—— O my Lord!—— I pray: Stay by my—— side;
—— be with me,—— Lord!——

2. Merciful and gracious Lord, slow to anger is your word;
   Blessed is your holy name.
   From the depths we cry to you, on our dryness pour your dew;
   guide the steps that stray so far without you! Be present, Lord!

3. So today we hear your voice, welcome you into our hearts;
   calling on your holy name.
   All in heaven, all on earth, hear the justice of your Word;
   save your holy people here below you! Be present Lord, O Lord!

Joe Mattingly
Text and music © 1994, Joe Mattingly

11 Bread of Life

1., 4. Bread of life, our con - so - la - tion.
2. Lamb of God, for all you suf - fered.
3. Word of God, O light e - ter - nal.

1., 4. Bread of life, our source of hope.
2. Lamb of God, you died and rose.
3. Word of God, foun - da - tion strong.

1., 4. Bread of life, our strength and cour - age.
2. Lamb of God, you'll come in glo - ry,
3. Word of God, re - sound with - in us,

1., 4. Bread of life, come make us one.
2. Lamb of God, to lead us home.
3. Word of God, for - ev - er - more.

Michael John Poirier
Text and music © 1992, Michael John Poirier

12 Build a Family

1. Different hearts, different lives, one in the name of God.
Different hurts, different needs, one goal, one mission,
building the kingdom of God.

REFRAIN

May— we be ho - ly in— our— lives,— may— we

shine bright - ly on— our— way,— and may we

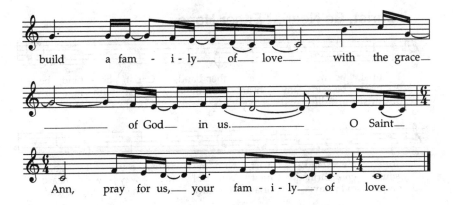

build a fam - i - ly___ of___ love___ with the grace___

_____ of God___ in us._____ O Saint___

Ann, pray for us,___ your fam - i - ly___ of love.

2. Spread the faith, spread the truth, open your heart to God.
If you fall, we will rise! We are one body,
one in the name of our God.

Ed Bolduc
Text and music © 1995, WLP

By the Waters of Babylon 13

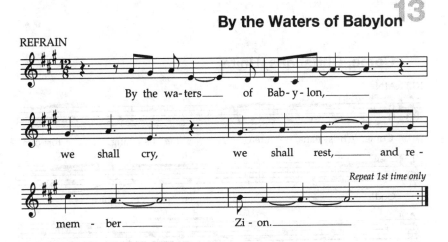

REFRAIN

By the wa - ters___ of Bab - y - lon,_____

we shall cry, we shall rest,___ and re -

Repeat 1st time only

mem - ber___ Zi - on._____

1. We long to play our harps and raise a song to you.
But how can we sing our song in a foreign land?

2. May we not forget beloved Jerusalem!
Lord, help us to sing our song in this foreign land!

3. Lord, we need your strength! Fill us with your spirit!
Inspire us to bring your song to this foreign land!

Paul A. Tate
Text and music © 1996, WLP

14 Christ, Be Near at Either Hand

1. Christ, be near at ei - ther hand, Christ, be - hind, be -
2. Christ, be in my heart and mind, Christ with - in__ my_
3. Christ my life and on - ly way, Christ my lan - tern_

1. fore me stand; Christ, with me where - e'er I go,
2. soul en - shrined; Christ, con - trol my way - ward heart;
3. night and day;__ Christ, be my un - chang - ing friend,

1. Christ, a - round, a - bove, be - low.
2. Christ, a - bide__ and__ ne'er de - part.
3. Guide and shep - herd to the end.

The Lorica of St. Patrick

Irish folk song

15 Come, Christians, Unite

REFRAIN
Cantor/All

Come, Chris-tians, u - nite._____ Let us sing_____ for our

God!_____ Come, peo - ple, re - joice!_____

Let us sing_____ for our God!_____

VERSES

1. The One who makes all things wor - thy,_____ the
2. The Lord of all____ cre - a - tion,_____ the
3. Come, fill our hearts with your good - ness;_____ come,

1. One who makes all things bright!
2. Lord, the giv - er of life!
3. fill our lives with new life!

1. Let us sing!
2. Let us sing!
3. Let us sing!

Ed Bolduc
Text and music © 1993, WLP

Come Home 16

1. Jesus tenderly is calling, calling out for you and me.
   Jesus patiently is waiting, waiting our return.

REFRAIN

Call - ing soft - ly_ and_ ten - der - ly,

Je - sus,_ for_ you_ and me. Soft - ly_ and_ ten -

- der-ly, Je - sus_ our Lord!_ Come home,_

_ come home._ Come home,_ come home._

2. Love so wonderful is promised, promised now for you and me.
   Though we've sinned, the Lord is merciful, merciful our Lord!

3. Jesus from the cross is pleading, pleading now for you and me.
   Should we linger without heeding the mercy of our Lord!

Will L. Thompson, 1847–1909, alt.

Joe Mattingly
Music © 1993, Joe Mattingly

17 Come! Let Us Sing Out Our Praise

REFRAIN

Cantor
Come! Let us sing out our praise to the Lord God of

Cantor
hosts!

All
Come! Let us sing out our praise to the Lord God of

Come! Let us sing out our praise to the Lord God of

hosts!

hosts!   *To Verses*

1. On
2. —
3. —

Come! Let us sing out our praise to the Lord God of

VERSES

Cantor
1. cym - bal and harp,___ the horn and the drum,___ give
2. Praise___ the Mak - er of heav - en and earth; give
3. We need not fear___ the dark - ness of night,___ for we're

All
hosts!

1. praise to our God! With
2. praise to our God!
3. nev - er a - lone!

1. glad tam - bou - rines, with the flute and the strings, pro -
2. Lift up the song with a voice proud and strong so that
3. God is the light that__ breaks through the night to il-

To Refrain
Last time to Final Refrain

1. claim the re - splend - ence of God!
2. e - ven the deaf ones will hear!
3. lu - mine our lives with his love!

FINAL REFRAIN

Cantor
Come! Let us sing out our praise to the Lord God of

Cantor
hosts!

All
Come! Let us sing out our praise to the Lord God of

Come! Let us sing out our praise to the Lord God of

hosts!

Cantor
hosts!

Paul A. Tate
Text and music © 1997, WLP

18 Come, Worship the Lord

REFRAIN

Come, and wor-ship the Lord, _____ for we are his peo - ple, the flock that he shep-herds. _____

(⌢) Last time

_____ Al - le - lu - ia. _____

VERSES 1, 2

1. Come, let us sing to the Lord, and shout with
2. Come, let us bow down and wor-ship, bend - ing the

1. joy _____ to the rock who saves us.
2. knee be-fore the Lord our Mak - er.

1. Let us come with thanks- giv - ing, and sing joy - ful
2. __ For we are his peo - ple, __ __ we are the

2. To Refrain

1. songs to the Lord. _____
2. flock that he shep-herds. _____

VERSE 3

3. The Lord is God, the might - y God, the
3. great king o'er all oth-er gods._____ He holds in his
3. hands the depths of the earth and the high - est
3. moun-tains as well. He made the sea, it be -
3. longs now to him; the dry land, too, was
3. formed by his hand._____

To Refrain

Ps 95

John Michael Talbot
Text and music © 1980, Birdwing Music/BMG Songs

19 Crux Fidelis

REFRAIN

Crux fi - de - lis; cross of glad - ness,

tree on which our hope is___ hung;

Let my arms be as your branch - es!

Yours, the song___ that___ must be___ sung.

VERSES

1. The Lord___ Je - sus loved us and
2. The Lord___ Je - sus en - tered the
3. To strive for jus - tice, e - ven when
4. We keep be - fore us that which our
5. The cup is poured out! So may we
6. The road in - vites us, marked with the

1. gave his life for us; few of us shall be
2. pain and death of sin. He ac - cept - ed the
3. stub - born - ness pre - vails to be one with the
4. kin - dred had of old: all the pain and the
5. drink as did our Lord, in this cup we are
6. steps of kin - dred past, they left foot - steps that

1. called to do the same. Yet all of us must
2. tor - ment of the cross. But with the cross he
3. des - p'rate of the world; To stand with those who
4. suf - f'ring of the cross. Yet where that cross is
5. called to share his fate. And let us not stand
6. spoke of heav - y loads. But they did not trudge

1.	lay	down	our	lives	a - long	with	his:	Let	the
2.	gave	us	the	bless - ed	gift	of	joy:	Let	the
3.	cry	out	when	we	can't bring	re -	lief:	Let	that
4.	plant -	ed,	the	seeds	of	hope	en - dure:	Let	that
5.	back	from	the	cross	to	which we're	called:	Let	the
6.	slow -	ly!	They	strode	a - long	this	path,	Our___	

To Refrain

1.	cross	be	our	com - pan - ion	as	we	dail - y	fol - low	him.
2.	cross	be	our	com - pan - ion	as	we	dail - y	fol - low	him.
3.	hope	be	our	com - pan - ion	as	we	dail - y	fol - low	him.
4.	hope	be	our	com - pan - ion,	as	we	dail - ly	fol - low	him.
5.	cross	be	our	com - pan - ion	as	we	dail - y	fol - low	him.
6.	on -	ly	hope	be - fore us,	as	we're	called	to	fol - low	him.

Text (vss.) adapt. from *Constitution of the Congregation of Holy Cross*

Steven C. Warner
Text (ref.) and music © 1996, WLP

20 Draw Near

REFRAIN

Cantor/All

Draw near, draw___ near! Take the bod - y
of your Lord. Draw near, draw___ near!
Drink the___ blood for you out-poured.

VERSES

Cantor

1. Draw near and take the bod - y of your Lord,
2. Christ, our Re - deem - er, God's e - ter - nal Son,
3. Let us ap - proach with faith - ful hearts sin - cere,
4. With heav'n - ly bread makes those who hun - ger whole,

1. And drink the ho - ly blood for you out-poured:
2. Has by his cross and blood the vic - t'ry won:
3. And take the pledg - es of sal - va - tion here:
4. Gives liv - ing wa - ters to the thirst - ing soul:

1. Saved by his bod - y and his ho - ly blood, With
2. He gave his life for great - est and for least, Him -
3. Christ, who in this life all the saints de - fends, Gives
4. Judge of the na - tions, to whom all must bow, In

To Refrain

1. souls re - freshed we give our thanks to God.
2. self the of - f'ring and him - self the Priest.
3. all be - liev - ers life that nev - er ends.
4. this great feast of love is with us now.

Sancti, venite, Christi corpus sumite
7th cent. hymn, tr. by John M. Neale, 1818–1866, alt.

Steven R. Janco
Music © 1992, WLP

REFRAIN

Cantor/All

Bread of life, sav-ing cup, feed our hun-gry souls with you. Nour-ish us, strength-en us; by your pres-ence in this meal may we be one. one.

Last time to Final ⌐3⌐   *To Verses* *Final*

Cantor

By your pres-ence in this meal may we be one.

All ⌐3⌐

VERSES

Cantor

1. Be - hold the Lamb of God,
2. Be - hold the meal of heav'n,
3. Be - hold the way of truth,
4. Be - hold the cov - e - nant,

All

Bread of life, sav-ing cup,

Cantor

1. Who takes a - way our sins,
2. A feast for rich and poor,
3. Our source of hope and peace,
4. The sac - ri - fice of Love,

All

Nour-ish us, strength-en us.

Cantor

1. We're blest and called to dine,
2. O Christ, our gra - cious host,
3. How great a gift of love,
4. The cup of last - ing life,

All

Bread of life, sav-ing cup,

Cantor

1. At the ban - quet of the Lord.
2. At the ban - quet of the Lord.
3. Our__ treas - ure and our joy.
4. Our__ prom - ise of your love.

All *To Refrain*

Nour-ish us, strength-en us.

Paul Hillebrand
Text and music © 1994, WLP

22 Friends

1. Pack- ing up__ the dreams God plant- ed
2. With the faith and love God's giv - en

1. In the fer - tile soil__ of you;__
2. Spring-ing from the hope we know,__

1. Can't be - lieve the hopes he's grant-ed Means a
2. We will pray the joy__ you'll live in __ __

1. chap - ter in__ your life__ is through.__
2. Is the strength that now__ you show.__

1.–2. But we'll keep you close_____ as al - ways; It won't e-

1.–2. - ven seem__ you've gone,__ 'Cause our hearts in big and

1.–2. small ways Will keep the love__ that keeps__ us strong.

1.–2. And__ friends are friends__ for - ev - er If the

1.–2. Lord's__ the Lord__ of them.__ And a

1.–2. friend will not__ say "nev - er" 'Cause the wel-come will__ not end.__

1.–2. Though it's hard to let___ you go,___ In the
1.–2. Fa - ther's hands___ we know___ That a
1.–2. life - time's not___ too long___ To live___ as friends.__

1.

To Verse 2 | 2. D.S.

And___

3.

___ No a life- time's not___ too long___

To live___ as friends.___

Michael W. Smith and Deborah D. Smith
Text and music © 1982, Meadowgreen Music Company

23 Fly Together

1. You and I, we live in a world where hope's in short supply,
   a world that's coming apart at the seams.
   It's a world of profit and loss, a world of winners and losers,
   a world that seems to want to crush our dreams.
   I'm standing here beside you, atop a lofty mountain,
   from which we've seen a world that might be one.
   The time has come for us to leave the mountain's shelter,
   to make a way between the earth and sun.
   We've got to...

REFRAIN

Fly____ to-geth-er:____ let that be our song;
Fly____ to-geth - er____ to help each one a - long,____
Fly____ to-geth - er, be - fore we fly a - part.
Fly to-geth - er this jour - ney of the heart.

2. There's another world we've seen where loss is shared and lessened,
   and profit is when everybody wins;
   faith's an open hand, and hope's your next-door neighbor;
   community's the way the dream begins.
   Thank you for the nest, and thank you for the nurture,
   thank you for the dream that in us sings.
   We shall find our way: you've given us direction,
   the courage and the strength to spread our wings.
   We've got to...

Rory Cooney
Text and music © 1998, WLP

Glorify the Lord with Me

REFRAIN

Glo - ri - fy the Lord with me! Let us to - geth - er ex -

Repeat first time only

alt God's name for - ev - er!

VERSES

1. I sought the Lord, and he an - swered me!
2. With all my heart I will thank the Lord,
3. God's might - y arm and his right - eous - ness
4. I shall sing praise to the might - y God

1. He de - liv - ered me from all my fears!
2. for how won - der - ful are all his deeds!
3. have re - leased me from my sin.
4. who has saved my soul from death!

1. Look to the Lord, so that you will be
2. Call on the Lord, for his mer - cy shall
3. Seek the Lord; be as - sured that God
4. Come and re - joice, for we have been

To Refrain, last time to Final Refrain

1. filled with his glo - ri - ous light!
2. last for all time, with - out end!
3. hears all who call on his name!
4. blessed with an un - sur - passed love!

To Final Refrain...

FINAL REFRAIN

Glo - ri - fy the Lord with me! Let us to-geth-er ex-

alt God's name for - ev - er!_____ Ex -

alt God's name_____ for - ev - er!_____

Paul A. Tate
Text and music © 1998, WLP

25 Gathered As One

VERSES

Cantor

1. Man - y fa - ces, the young and the old,_
2. Man - y pil - grims,_____ shar - ing at feast,
3. Man - y voic - es,_____ raised up in song,

All

1.–3. gath - ered as one in our God!

Cantor

1. Through-out his - t'ry the sto - ry's re - told,
2. All are wel - come the great - est and least,
3. In one fam - 'ly where all can be - long,

All

1.–3. gath - ered as one in our God!_____ *Cantor* Like

1.–3. those come be-fore_ us, we lis - ten and learn._ We re -

1.–3. mem- ber the prom - ise and a - wait your re- turn.— So with-

1.–3. out hes - i - ta - tion a new gen- er - a - tion pro-

1.–3. claims the sal - va - tion of God!

REFRAIN

All

Gath- ered as one— in Je - sus your Son,—

lift-ing our voic-es in praise,— we know and be- lieve and

long to re - ceive— the bread that is strength for our

1.–2.

days, gath- ered as one!

To Verses 2

Final

one!

Paul A. Tate and Deanna Light
Text and music © 1997, WLP

26 Go Light Your World

1. There is a candle in every soul; some brightly burning,
   some dark and cold.
   There is a Spirit who brings a fire,
   ignites a candle and makes his home.

REFRAIN

1.–4. So, car-ry your can - dle, run to the dark-ness,

1. seek out the hope - less, con-fused and torn.
2. seek out the lone - ly, the tired and worn.
3. seek out the help - less, de-ceived and poor.
4. seek out the hope - less, con-fused and torn.

1.–4. Hold out your can - dle for all to see it.

1.–4. Take your can-dle and go light your world. Take your

1.
1. can-dle and go light your world.

To Verse 2

2.
2. can-dle and go light your world.

To Verse 3

3.
3. can - dle and go light your world.

Repeat Refrain

4.
4. can - dle

4. and go light your world. Take your can-dle

4. and go light your world. Mmm Mmm

2. Frustrated brother, see how he's tried to light
   his own candle some other way.
   See now your sister, she's been robbed and lied to,
   still holds a candle without a flame.

3. We are a family whose hearts are blazing,
   so let's raise our candles and light up the sky.
   Praying to our Father, in the name of Jesus,
   make us a beacon in darkest time.

Chris Rice
Text and music © 1993, BMG Songs, Inc. (ASCAP)

27 God So Loved the World

REFRAIN

God so loved the world that he gave his on - ly Son that who- ev - er be-lieves in him shall nev - er die,_____ but have e - ter - nal life._____

VERSES 1, 2

1. God did not send the Son in - to the world
2. God sent a ho - ly light in - to the world,

1. to con - demn the world, but that the
2. and we sought the dark, but Je - sus

To Refrain

1. world might be saved through him!_____ Yes,
2. calls us to fol - low him._____ Yes,

VERSE 3

3. All who seek the truth, come in - to the light! Make

To Refrain

3. clear that your deeds are done in God!_____ Yes,

Paul A. Tate
Text and music © 1998, WLP

REFRAIN

All

This is the bread that came down from heav - en, bro-ken for

all as gift of God's grace. Food from the earth be -

comes blood and bod - y; God's ho - ly mys-t'ry,_____ re -

vealed in this place._____

VERSES

All

1.–4. Je - sus tells his dis - ci - ples,_____

Cantor

1. "I am hope for all who be - lieve in me."_____
2. "All who eat this bread shall__ nev - er die."_____
3. "All who come to me shall__ nev - er thirst."_____
4. "I will raise you up on the last__ day."_____

All

1.–4. Je - sus tells his dis - ci - ples,_____

To Refrain

1.–4. "Come and fol - low me and live!"_____

5. Come, taste the bread of new birth!
    Come, drink the wine of everlasting life,
    broken and poured out that the world might live!

Paul A. Tate
Text and music © 1998, WLP

29 God's Love Is Eternal

Paul A. Tate
Text and music © 1995, WLP

REFRAIN

Praise God the Fa-ther and God the Son! Praise God the
Spir-it, Three - in - One! Praise God who has been, who
is, and will be! Praise the Al - might - y,
Great One in Three!

VERSES

1. Help us to lis - ten, Teach-er of all, o - pen our
2. Give us new vi - sion, Spir - it of fire; we are the
3. Al - pha, O - me - ga, the first and the last, you know our

1. hearts to an - swer your call. In - spire us to
2. proph-ets you move and in - spire. Re - store us to
3. fu - ture, our pres - ent, our past. Be with us

1. love and fill us with grace un - til we see
2. joy from death to re - birth as we work for your
3. now and all of our days, and we shall ex -

To Refrain

1. you face to face!
2. king - dom on earth!
3. alt you with praise!

Paul A. Tate and Paul L. Berrell
Text and music © 1998, WLP

31 Harbor of My Heart

Har-bor of my heart, I take ref - uge in you, Pre -

serve me, O God! My joy is in you a - lone.

1. Preserve me, O God, my Savior;
   I take refuge within your embrace.
   I say to the Lord, "You are my God.
   My joy alone is found in you."

2. He has put into my heart a wondrous love
   for the faithful who dwell in your land.
   It is you, O Lord, who are my cup,
   you alone, my portion and my prize.

3. My destiny, O Lord, is my delight;
   how I welcome your will for me!
   I will bless the Lord who gives me counsel,
   who at night is the compass of my heart.

4. The pathway of my life will be shown to me,
   the fullness of joy in your presence.
   At your side, my soul will sing forever,
   to the One who brought life unto my spirit.

Ps 16: 1–2, 5, 7, 11

Steven C. Warner
Text and music © 1995, WLP

32 He Is Exalted

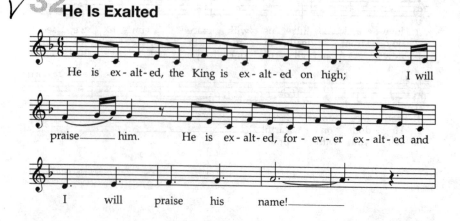

He is ex - alt - ed, the King is ex - alt - ed on high; I will

praise___ him. He is ex - alt - ed, for - ev - er ex - alt - ed and

I will praise his name!_____

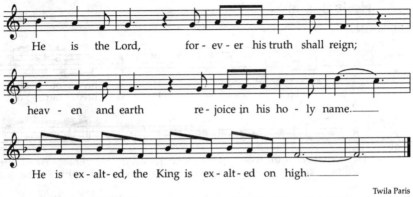

He is the Lord, for-ev-er his truth shall reign; heav-en and earth re-joice in his ho-ly name. He is ex-alt-ed, the King is ex-alt-ed on high.

Twila Paris
Text and music © 1985, Straightway Music/Mountain Spring Music

He Answers All Our Needs

33

REFRAIN
Cantor/All

The hand of the Lord feeds us. The hand of the Lord feeds us. The hand of the Lord feeds us. He an-swers all our needs.

(⌢) Last Time

VERSES
Cantor

1. Faith-ful is the Lord who loves his peo-ple.
2. Gra-cious is the Lord and slow to an-ger.
3. Right-eous is the Lord, our lov-ing Fa-ther.

1. Faith-ful is our Lord who up-holds all those who bow be-
2. Gra-cious is our Lord who has shown com-pas-sion for his
3. Ho-ly is our Lord who is al-ways near to those who

To Refrain

1. fore him. He's our Lord! We are glad!
2. peo-ple. He is Lord! We are glad!
3. call him. He's our Lord! We are glad!

Based on Ps 145
Text (ref.) © 1969, 1981, ICEL

Ed Bolduc
Text (vss.) and music © 1993, 1997, WLP

34 He Is Jesus

REFRAIN

His name is Je - sus! He is Christ our— Lord!
——— He's Je - sus! He is Christ our— Lord!

He's al-ways with us! He's our re - deem - ing— Lord! He is our
He'll nev - er leave us! Christ,— the Sav - ior— born to be our

sav - ing— grace in this chang-ing world.—
sav - ing— grace in this chang-ing world.—

(⌢) Last time

VERSES

1. The peo - ple have seen a great light,
2. — Lift up your heads, O you— gates.

1. all those who dwell in the land of shad - ows.
2. O - pen your hearts to the King of Glo - ry.

1. Na - tions are filled with new— joy. Such is the joy we
2. He holds the Spir - it of— God, wis - dom of life and

1. sing be - fore— you. O ho - ly— God,—
2. un - der - stand - ing. O ho - ly— God,—

1. send this light in - to our— world. O
2. send your love in - to our— world. O

1. ho - ly— God,——— send this light in - to our world.
2. ho - ly— Lord,——— bring your love in - to our world.

Ed Bolduc
Text and music © 1992, WLP

Hear Me, O God

REFRAIN

Hear me, O God. Hear me, O God. I

place my trust in you.———

VERSES

1. Lis - ten to my prayer—— and save me, for
2. Lord,— let your love come up - on me; you
3. I shall walk the path of your free - dom and
4. I am friend to all—— who praise you, who
5. How long must your serv - ant suf - fer? When

1. night will soon be here! Be the light that
2. are my sav - ing help! I shall keep your
3. seek to know your ways! I shall wor - ship
4. long to know your love! Let my heart be
5. will you judge my foes? I will al - ways

1. shat - ters my de - spair.———
2. law for - ev - er - more.———
3. you, the God I trust.———
4. blame - less in your sight.———
5. long to do your will.———

Paul A. Tate
Text and music © 1998, WLP

36 Here I Am, O God

REFRAIN

Cantor/All

Here I am, O God, I come to do your will, I come to do your will.

To Verses

VERSES

Cantor

1. ___ I ___ wait-ed for the Lord, and my
2. A ___ new song was put in-to my mouth, a ___
3. How ___ man - y, O Lord, ___ my ___ God, are your
4. It is writ - ten with-in the Ho - ly Word, that ___

1. Mak - er bent down to hear me. My ___ cry and my
2. hymn of my Cre - a - tor; for the man - y shall
3. won - ders and your de- signs! ___ The ___ mar - vels you
4. I should do your will. ___ In the depths of my

To Refrain

1. prayer were heard in the heart of God.
2. see and trust in the Lord, our God.
3. work are great be - yond all praise.
4. heart I sing be - fore your Word.

Steven C. Warner
Text and music © 1993, WLP

Holy Is His Name

VERSES

1. My soul__ pro-claims the great-ness of the Lord,__
2. He has mer-cy_____ in ev-'ry gen-er-a-tion.

1. __ and my spir-it_____ ex-alts in God my Sav-ior.
2. He has__ re-vealed_____ his pow-er and his glo-ry.

1. For he has looked_ with mer-cy on my low-li-ness,
2. He has cast down__ the might-y in their ar-ro-gance,

1. and my name__ will be for-ev-er ex-alt-ed.
2. and has lift-ed up__ the meek and the low-ly.

1. For the might-y God_ has done great things for me,__
2. He has come to help_ his serv-ant Is-ra-el;__

1. __ and his mer-cy_____ will reach from age to age.__
2. he__ re-mem-bers__ his prom-ise to our fa-thers.

REFRAIN

And__ ho - ly, ho - ly,

ho - ly is his__ name._____

John Michael Talbot
Text and music © 1980, Birdwing Music/BMG Songs, Inc.

38 Holy You

1. Though the seas sweep up to drown us,
   evil faces close around us,
   and the only sound to guide us
   is the falling of our tears,
   though our throats are parched and aching,
   and our hearts are quailing, breaking,
   like a flame does utter darkness,
   you have banished all our fears.

REFRAIN

Ho - ly you, might - y you, we place all our trust in you._____ You con-sume____ us, you re-deem us: set us free, and we will try to be like you.

2. Though they feed us words like poison
   for the faith that we have chosen,
   sink us deep into a mire
   so we have nowhere left to run,
   they insult us for our praying,
   for we never cease our saying
   that you pardoned all our sin
   before we knew what we had done.

VERSE 3

3. Ho - ly you!_____ You sur - prise us by your giv - ing. Ho - ly you!_____ You are faith-ful to your own.

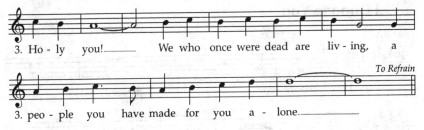

3. Ho - ly you!___ We who once were dead are liv - ing, a

3. peo - ple you have made for you a - lone.___

To Refrain

Rory Cooney and Claire Cooney
Text and music © 1998, WLP

I Am the Bread of Life **39**

REFRAIN

I___ am the___ bread of life.___ All who
I___ am God's love re - vealed. I am

eat this bread will nev - er die.___ —
bro - ken___ that you might be healed.___ —

1.   2. *To Verses*

VERSES

1. All who eat___ of this heav - en - ly bread,
2. No one who comes to me___ shall ev - er hun - ger a - gain.

1. — All who drink this cup of the
2. — No one who be - lieves___ shall ev - er

1. cov - e - nant,___ you will live for -
2. thirst.___ All that the Fa - ther draws shall

To Refrain

1. ev - er, for— I will raise you up.___
2. come to me and I will give them rest.___

John Michael Talbot
Text and music © 1982, Birdwing Music / BMG Songs

40 I Choose You

REFRAIN

I choose you. I choose you.

You shall be the way,

You shall be the truth. I choose

you. I choose you. Be the road

be-tween my peo-ple and my dreams.

1. I am the words you drink, written in spirit and flame;
   I am the words that reach you, trying to teach you my name.

2. I am the tongue of fire that lights up with love in your eyes.
   I am the glimmer in your heart not to grow dimmer and die!

3. I am the walls around you, the castle that keeps you from harm.
   I am the the arms that hold you, you'll never be cold in my arms!
   I am your dreams, I am all of your dreams, the keeper of your safety.
   I am the weaver of your dreams.

4. I choose you, I choose you, my disciple, my beloved child.
   My eyes, my arms, my truth, my shelter,
   the tongue of flame still burning from your dreams.
   My love that flows within you through your dreams,
   the road between my people and my dreams.

Rory Cooney and Claire Cooney
Text and music © 1998, WLP

I Rejoiced When I Heard Them Say 41

REFRAIN

Cantor/All

I re- joiced when I heard them say, let us go to the house of the Lord! Al- le- lu - ia, al - le - lu - ia!

VERSES

Cantor

1. I re - joiced when I heard them say: "Let us
2. O Je - ru - sa - lem built as a cit - y, as a
3. They come to praise the Lord. For

4. For the peace of Je - ru - sa - lem pray: "May your
5. For the love of my fam - 'ly and friends, I say:
6. Praise the Fa - ther, the Son, and Spir - it both

1. go to the house of the Lord." And
2. ci - ty u - nit - ed and strong! It is
3. Is - ra - el's law it is. The

4. homes fill with peace and pros - per!" May
5. "Peace of the Lord be up - on you." For the
6. now and for - ev - er - more. To the

1. now our feet are stand - ing with - in your
2. here that the tribes go to - geth - er, the
3. thrones of judg - ment are set there, with - in the

4. peace find a home in your dwell - ings, with - in your
5. love of the house of the Lord I will
6. God who brings life to our be - ing, from

To Refrain

1. gates, O Je - ru - sa - lem.
2. tribes of the Lord our God.
3. walls of the house of Da - vid.

4. walls may God's peace en - dure.
5. ask for your good.
6. now 'til the end of time.

Ps 122

Steven C. Warner
Text and music © 1994, WLP

42 I Have Been Anointed

REFRAIN

I have been a-noint - ed with the song of the Lord!

— A song of love and com-pas - sion, a song to set_ me_

free! God is my rock of sal-va - tion! A

bea - con for_ my_ soul! Hal - le - lu - jah! A - men!

Hal - le - lu - jah! A - men. Praise to the rock and the well-

1.

2.–3. To Verse

- spring, cre - a - tor of_ my_ soul! Oh, soul!

VERSE

My heart knew dark - ness, My soul was

filled with de-spair,— Life-less and si - lent, no

mu - sic an - y - where, and then my Lord and com-pan-

- ion, He filled my wait - ing_ soul: Hal - le - lu -

jah! Hal - le - lu - jah! For God has made— me— whole!

Steven C. Warner
Text and music © 1997, WLP

I Turn To You 43

REFRAIN

I turn to— you— in times of— need;—

To Verses, last time to Final

you fill me— with— your— joy!

VERSES

1.–3. Be glad, re - joice—— with all— your heart!—

1.–3. You fill my soul—— with peace,— O Lord.—

1. All our days— are filled with, All our nights— are filled with,
2. All our fear— you take a, All our doubt— you take a,
3. Hap - py— shall— your spir - it, Hap - py— shall— your spir - it,

To Refrain

1. All our lives— are filled with joy!—————
2. All our pain— you take a - way.————
3. Hap - py— shall— your spir - it— be.————

FINAL

Re - joice be glad!— With all your heart!— Re - joice!

Joe Mattingly
Text and music © 1994, WLP

REFRAIN

And I,— Lord, I will praise your name,— I'll sing,—
"You are my God and King."— For- ev-
- er you are al-might-y!

Repeat Refrain first time only

VERSE 1

1. Oh, I'll give you glo- ry,— my God and King,—
1. — and I'll bless your name— for- ev-
1. - er.— Oh, I'll bless you day af - ter day, and
1. I will praise your name— for- ev- er!—

To Refrain

VERSE 2

2. The Lord— is kind— and full of com- pas-sion,—
2. — slow— to an - ger,— rich— in love.—

2. ___ How good are you, Lord, to all,___ How

2. good are you, Lord, to all___ your crea- tures!___

VERSE 3

3. I will praise your name!___ I will praise your name

3. ___ for- ev- er! I will praise your name,___ my

3. King and my God!___ For- ev- er!

Ed Bolduc
Text and music © 1998, WLP

45 If Today You Hear the Voice of God

REFRAIN

If to-day,— if to-day____ you— hear the voice of

God, o-pen up____ your heart____ and

lis-ten to his— Word. If to-day,____ if to-day—

____ you— hear the voice of God,____ hard-en not your

hearts,____ hard-en not your— hearts.____

VERSES

1. Come, sing your joy to the Lord,— give praise to the God who
2. Come, let us wor-ship the Lord,— come, bow to the God who

1. saves us.— O come, give— thanks to the Lord,— come
2. made us,— for we are the sheep of his land,— the

1. sing be-fore our God.
2. flock led by his hand. He is the Lord of our lives,____

To Refrain

1.–2. — he is the Lord of our lives and we pray.____

Ed Bolduc
Text and music © 1998, WLP

In Remembrance of You

VERSES

1. Je - sus, hope for all, teach us to be-
2. Je - sus, Son of God, you are liv - ing
3. Je - sus, Lamb of God, bear - er of our

1. lieve. Reach us, hope for all,_____ in
2. Word. Teach us, Son of God,_____ to
3. sin, Free us, Lamb of God;_____ come

1. wa - ter, wine, and wheat._____
2. share what we have heard._____
3. heal us from with - in._____

REFRAIN

Gath - ered at ta - ble, gath - ered in love, food for the jour - ney

sent from a - bove. Strength - en and feed us in all that we do,

gath - ered at ta - ble in re - mem - brance of you.

To Verses | *Final*

you. Gath - ered at ta - ble_____

2

____ in re - mem - brance of you.

Paul A. Tate
Text and music © 1997, WLP

47 In the Arms of the Shepherd

REFRAIN

In the arms of the Shep - herd___ will my long - ing find con - tent - ment; in the arms of the Shep - herd___ will my jour - ney find an end.___

To Verses

VERSE 1

1. The Lord of life is the Shep-herd__ who has giv-en me all that I need; wa-ters of peace and pas-tures of green re-fresh my wea - ry heart.___ Though dark of night may sur-round me,___ I will nev - er give in to fear. You will show me the path and walk by my side, pro - tect - ing me from harm.

2 To Refrain

VERSE 2

2. You have set a boun - ti - ful ta - ble___ in the sight of those who would harm me; fill - ing my cup, you

2. hon - or me as be - lov - ed guest. You have

2. prom - ised your love and your kind - ness____ to be

2. with me as long as I live, your house will be my

2 *To Refrain*

2. home for all the days of my life.

Marcy Weckler
Text and music © 1995, WLP

In the Light **48**

1.–3. In the light_____ of the Lord_____ we are

1. one,_____ we are chil - dren._____
2. strong_____ in our weak - ness._____
3. healed_____ of our blind - ness._____

1.–3. In the light_____ of the Lord_____ we are

1. one,_____ we are one,_____ we are one,_____
2. strong,_____ we are strong,_____ we are strong,_____
3. healed,_____ we are healed,_____ we are healed,_____

1. __ we are one._____
2. __ we are strong._____
3. __ we are healed._____

Michael John Poirier
Text and music © 1986, Michael John Poirier

49 In You, O Lord

1. In you, O Lord, I have found my
2. In you, O Lord, I have found my

1. peace. In you, O Lord, I have found my
2. strength. In you, O Lord, I have found my

1. joy. I cry un-to you and you lead me
2. hope. I cry un-to you and you hear my

1.
1. home. You are peace, you are joy, you are God.
2. voice. You are strength, you are hope, you are

Final
God. I cry un-to you and you lead me

home. You are peace, you are joy, you are God.

Text (lines 1 and 2) © 1969, 1981, ICEL

Ed Bolduc
Additional text and music © 1998, WLP

50 Journey for Home

VERSES

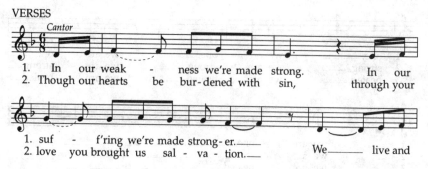

Cantor

1. In our weak - ness we're made strong. In our
2. Though our hearts be bur-dened with sin, through your

1. suf - f'ring we're made strong-er. We live and
2. love you brought us sal - va - tion.

1.–2. jour-ney, jour-ney for home.

In the
Through the

1. dark we turn to the light. In our faith you heal our
2. gifts and love that we share, we will know your pres-ence a-

1. blind-ness
2. mong us. We live and jour-ney, jour-ney for home.

REFRAIN

All

And may we glo-ri-fy your name as we re-new our love each

day. Lord, make us strong in hope and faith, we sing to you.

For it is you who draws us here, our Lord, Mes-si-ah, al-ways

1.

To Verses

near. We live and jour-ney, jour-ney for home.

2.

home. We live and jour-ney, jour-ney for home.

Ed Bolduc
Text and music © 1998, WLP

51 Let All Creation Sing Alleluia

REFRAIN

Let all cre-a-tion
sing al - le-lu - ia!
Let all cre-a-tion
sing al - le-lu - ia! In one heart and voice let all

(⌢) Last time

crea - tures re-joice in God!

VERSES

1. All crea-tures of our God and King
2. O rush-ing wind and breez-es soft,
3. O flow-ing wa - ter, pure and clear,
4. O ev - 'ry - one of ten - der heart,
5. Let all things their Cre - a - tor bless

Cantor simile

1. All crea-tures of our God and King
2. O rush-ing wind and breez-es soft,
3. O flow-ing wa - ter, pure and clear,
4. O ev - 'ry - one of ten - der heart,
5. Let all things their Cre - a - tor bless

1. Lift up your voice and with us sing!
2. O clouds that ride the winds a - loft,
3. Make mu - sic for your Lord to hear.
4. For - giv - ing oth - ers, take your part.
5. And wor - ship God in hum - ble - ness.

1. O burn - ing sun with gold - en beam
2. O ris - ing morn in praise re - joice,
3. O fire so mas - ter - ful and bright,
4. All you who pain and sor - row bear,
5. Oh, praise the Fa - ther, praise the Son,

									To Refrain
1.	—	And	sil - ver	moon	with	soft - er	gleam!
2.	—	O	lights	of	eve - ning	find	a	voice!
3.	—	Pro - vid - ing	us	with	warmth and	light!
4.	—	Praise God	and	cast	on	God your	care!
5.	—	And praise	the	Spir - it,	Three - in - One!

Based on Francis of Assisi, 1182–1226
Tr. by William H. Draper, 1855–1933, alt.
Text © 1923, 1927 (Renewed), J. Curwen & Sons, Ltd.

Paul A. Tate
Music © 1998, WLP

Lay Down That Spirit   52

REFRAIN

Send down your Spir- it, Lord,— lay down your
Word, O Lord,— send down your Spir- it, Lord,— and re-
new the face of the earth.

Repeat first time only

VERSES

1. Bless the Lord!—   You are great in - deed!—
2. Earth and sky!—   From the moun - tain top!—

1. O my soul!
2. Praise the Lord!

1.–2. With maj - es - ty and with awe,

1. Great in - deed!
2. Shout the Word!   O

1.–2. with maj - es - ty and with awe, we praise you,

To Refrain

1.–2. Lord,———   O Lord, O Lord!

Ps 104

Joe Mattingly
Text and music © 1993, WLP

53 Let the Fire Fall

VERSES

1.–3. Ho - ly Spir - it, Ho - ly Spir - it,_____

1. Come___ with___ your fire!___ Ho - ly Spir - it,
2. pu - ri - fy___ my heart!___ Ho - ly Spir - it,
3. set my life___ on fire!___ Ho - ly Spir - it,

1. Ho - ly Spir - it,_____ come___ with your fire!___
2. Ho - ly Spir - it,_____ pu - ri - fy___ my heart!
3. Ho - ly Spir - it,_____ set my life___ on fire!___

1. Ho - ly Spir - it, come___ with your fire!_____
2. Ho - ly Spir - it, pu - ri - fy my heart!_____
3. Ho - ly Spir - it, set my life on fire!_____

1. Ho - ly Spir - it, come___ with your fire!_____
2. Ho - ly Spir - it, pu - ri - fy my heart!_____
3. Ho - ly Spir - it, set my life on fire!_____

REFRAIN

Come, Ho - ly Spir - it.___ Let the fi - re fall!___

Let the fi - re fall!_____ Let the fi - re fall!_____

George Misulia
Text and music © 1984, Crossroads Music

Let Us Sing 54

REFRAIN

Let us sing,_____ let us sing___ a new song___
_ un - to the_ Lord!_ Let God's name_ for- ev - er be praised
_ in all_ the earth!_____ For the Lord
_ is our strength,_ and the Lord_ is our sal - va -
- tion._ So lift your voice_ and let us sing!_

1. How many times have I fallen, and my Lord, he has rescued me?
   Lifts me up when I'm down and out. You see, my Lord believes in me.

2. How many times have I called him, and my Lord, he has answered me?
   Hears my cry when I shout it out! You see, my Lord believes in me.

3. When I call his name, my Lord is there for me.
   When he calls my name, I know he'll set me free.
   When I call his name, my Lord is there for me.
   When he calls my name, I know he'll set me free.
   Set me free! Set me free!

Ed Bolduc
Text and music © 1998, WLP

VERSES

1. I am the vine,— you are the branch - es.—
2. You are the vine,— we are the branch - es.—

1. — I live in you and you— in me.
2. — We live in you and you— in us.

1. — Turn to me,———— I am the keep - er—
2. We turn to you,———— you are the keep - er—

1. ———— of the world.————
2. ———— of us all.————

REFRAIN

1. Live in me, I'll live— in you— and my words will stay
2. Live in me, I'll live— in you— and your words speak ev -

1. — with you. Ask what you will———— of— me.————
2. - er true. Ask what you will———— of— me.————

1. I am glo - ri - fied— in you in your bear - ing of—
2. You are glo - ri - fied— in me, where I go and when

1. — this fruit. You are my child— for - ev -
2. — I speak. I am your child— for - ev -

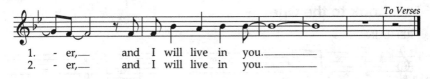

Ed Bolduc
Text and music © 1998, WLP

Lift Your Hearts to the Holy One

Deanna Light and Paul A. Tate
Text and music © 1998, WLP

57 Look to the One

REFRAIN

Look to the One, look to the One,

look to the One who comes in glo - ry!

1. He will be our light, he will turn the night into day. Jesus. Jesus.
   He will be our Lord, he will turn all sorrow to joy. Jesus. Jesus.
   Sing to the Lord! Bless his name! Praise him above the nations!

2. He will come with power, he will rule all nations on earth. Jesus. Jesus.
   He will shepherd all, he will take his flock in his arms. Jesus. Jesus.
   Sing to the Lord! Bless his name! Praise him above the nations!

3. A voice cries out! A voice cries out! A voice cries out:
   "Prepare ye the way!"

Ed Bolduc
Text and music © 1993, WLP

58 Lord, You Are Good

REFRAIN

Lord, you are good and for - giv - ing,_____

Lord, you are good and for - giv - ing._____

1. O Lord, full of love, incline your ear to us. O Lord, O Lord!

2. Nations sing your praise, for you alone are God. O Lord, O Lord!

3. You, O Lord, are grace; slow to anger, full of love. O Lord, O Lord!

Text (ref.) © 1969, 1981, ICEL

Ed Bolduc
Text (vss.) and music © 1993, WLP

Lord, Bless Your People

REFRAIN

Cantor/All

Lord, bless your peo - ple; Lord bless your

To Verses

peo - ple with peace, with the gift of your peace.

VERSES

Cantor

1. O give the Lord, you chil - dren of our God,
2. The voice of God, re - sound-ing on the wa - ters,
3. The voice of God breaks Le - ba - non's great ce - dars,
4. God's glo - ry breaks like thun - der in the moun-tains;

1. O give the Lord great glo - ry and pow - er,
2. The voice of God, im - mense on the seas!
3. God's voice re - sounds, and shat - ters the trees!
4. With - in the tem - ple are cries of great glo - ry!

1. O give the Lord a name filled with glo - ry,
2. The voice of God, re - splen - dent with pow - er,
3. God's voice will flash, like fire new - ly kin - dled,
4. Our God pre - sides o'er the depths of the wa - ters,

To Refrain

1. A - dore the Lord in a sa - cred place.
2. The song of God, full of splen - dor and might.
3. The song of God fills the wil - der - ness.
4. The Lord pre - sides for - ev - er - more.

Steven C. Warner
Text and music © 1995, WLP

60 Lord, I Lift Your Name on High

Lord, I lift your name on high; Lord, I love to sing__ your prais - es. I'm so glad you're in__ my life; I'm so glad you came__ to save__ us. You came from heav - en to earth__ to show the way,__ From the earth__ to the cross__ my debt to pay;__ From the cross__ to the grave,__ from the grave__ to the sky;__ Lord, I lift your name__ on high.

Rick Founds
Text and music © 1989, Maranatha! Music

Lord, You Have the Words

61

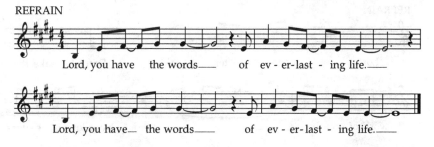

REFRAIN

Lord, you have the words— of ev-er-last-ing life.—

Lord, you have— the words— of ev-er-last-ing life.—

1. The law of the Lord is perfect, it revives the soul.
   The rule of the Lord is to be trusted, it gives wisdom to the simple.

2. The precepts of the Lord are right, they gladden the heart.
   The command of the Lord is clear, it gives light to the eyes.

3. The fear of the Lord is holy, abiding forever.
   The decress of the Lord are truth, and all ot them just.
   They are more to be desired than gold, than the purest gold.

Text (ref.) © 1969, 1981, ICEL
Text (vss.) © 1963, Ladies of the Grail, (England). GIA, exclusive agent.

Ed Bolduc
Music © 1998, WLP

Lord, You Have the Words of Everlasting Life

62

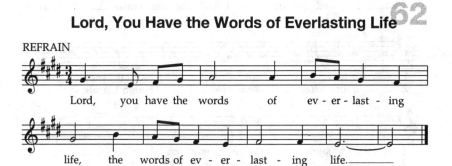

REFRAIN

Lord, you have the words of ev - er - last - ing

life, the words of ev - er - last - ing life.——

1. The law of the Lord is perfect, refreshing the soul;
   The decree of the Lord is trustworthy, giving wisdom to the simple.

2. The precepts of the Lord are right, rejoicing the heart;
   The command of the Lord is clear, enlightening the eye.

3. The fear of the Lord is pure, enduring forever;
   The ordinances of the Lord are true, all of them just.

4. They are more precious than gold, than a heap of purest gold;
   Sweeter also than syrup or honey from the comb.

Text (ref.) © 1969, 1981, ICEL
Text (vss.) © 1970, CCD

Marty Haugen
Music © 1987, WLP

63 Lord, Your Love Is Eternal

REFRAIN

Lord, your love is e-ter-nal. Don't for-sake the work of your hands._____ Lord, your love is e-ter-nal._____ Don't for-sake the work of your hands.

(⌢) Last time

VERSES

1. I will wor-ship you,_____ O Lord,_____ with song_____ and heart.__ I will sing your praise,_____ O Lord,_____ for you_____ are God.__ All the ends of the earth_____ shall know that you are God!_____

2. See__ how the Lord__ re-gards_____ the low-ly ones.__ He will nev-er raise_____ the proud_____ or draw_____ them near.__ Though I walk in these trou-bled times, you're with me, Lord._____

To Refrain

Text (ref.) © 1969, 1981, ICEL

Ed Bolduc
Text (vss.) and music © 1993, WLP

Make Us a Eucharistic People

1. Make us____ a Eu - cha - rist - ic peo - ple____ in
2. Make us____ a Gos - pel - liv - ing peo - ple____ in
3. Make us____ a king-dom-seek-ing peo - ple____ in
4. Make us____ a res - ur - rec-tion peo - ple____ in
5. Make us____ a jus - tice - lov-ing peo - ple____ in

1.–5. ev - 'ry-thing we are. Make us____ an ev - er-last-ing gift. With

1.–5. grate-ful hearts we lift a song of our thanks-giv-ing. A- men.____

Julie and Tim Smith
Text and music © 1990, Troubador Pub.

May We and God Be One

REFRAIN

In the name of the rest - ful Fa - ther, in the

name of the calm - ing Son, in the name of the peace - ful

Spir - it,____ may we and God be one.____

1. I place my soul and body under your guarding this night, O God.
   O Father of help to lost children, protector of heaven and earth!

2. I place my soul and body under your guiding this night, O Christ.
   O Son of the tears and the piercings, tonight may your cross be my shield!

3. I place my soul and body under your glowing this night, O Spirit.
   O gentle companion and my soul's guardian, my heart's eternal fire!

Based on a Celtic prayer

Paul A. Tate
Text and music © 1988, WLP

66 May You Cling to Wisdom

REFRAIN

May you cling to wis-dom, for she will pro-tect you,

and if you cher-ish her, she will keep you safe.

1. Take heed, my children, and listen to my words,
   and all your years shall be rich and filled with joy.
   For I have taught you in ways of wisdom and paths of honesty.

2. More than all else, set a guard upon your heart,
   since here is found the wellspring of your soul!
   Upon your journey, let wisdom grace you with steadfast vision.

3. So may you treasure the things I have to say.
   These words of truth shall lead you both to life!
   Pray for perception, hold fast to wisdom, do not forget her!

Prv 4
Adapt. by S.C.W.

Steven C. Warner
Text and music © 1993, WLP

Most Wonderful Father

67

REFRAIN

You give "al - might - y" to your name.— Fa - ther of all, hear us pro-claim:——— "In ev-'ry land you've set us— free; you are al - might-y!"——————

VERSE

You are most won - der-ful, ho - ly Prince of Peace. O———— you are most won - der-ful,— might - y King of kings. Hear us, O Fa - ther, fill us with your love. O—— teach us, a - wak - en us,— show us how to love. O—— ho - ly,— ho - ly, ho - ly

To Refrain

is your—— name. O—— Lord, we— praise you!——

Ed Bolduc
Text and music © 1993, WLP

68 On That Holy Mountain

Cantor

1. The wolf___ is the guest___ of the lamb,___
2. The poor___ shall re - ceive___ from the rich,___
3. ___ Jus - tice shall flow'r for all time,

All   *Cantor*

1. on that ho - ly moun - tain.___ And the calf and the lion___
2. on that ho - ly moun - tain.___ And the sick and the lame
3. on that ho - ly moun - tain.___ ___ As long as the sun___

All

1. ___ shall lie down, on that ho - ly moun - tain.
2. ___ shall be healed, on that ho - ly moun - tain.
3. ___ still can shine, on that ho - ly moun - tain.

Cantor

1. To - geth - er___ they shall rest with the___ child,
2. The wick - ed___ shall be slain by God's___ breath,
3. ___ Peace___ till the moon be no___ more,

All

1. on that ho - ly moun - tain, on that ho - ly moun - tain,
2. on that ho - ly moun - tain, on that ho - ly moun - tain,
3. on that ho - ly moun - tain, on that ho - ly moun - tain,

1. on that ho - ly moun - tain of the Lord.___
2. on that ho - ly moun - tain of the Lord.___
3. on that ho - ly moun - tain of the Lord.___

REFRAIN

No harm or ruin___ on that ho-ly moun-tain.___

That sa-cred day___ shall be filled with knowl-edge.

There shall be peace,___ led by all the chil-dren,

on that ho-ly moun-tain,___ on that ho-ly moun-

Last time to Coda ⊕

- tain,___ on that ho-ly moun-tain___ of the Lord.

To Verses

⊕ **CODA**

2

Ho-ly and

peace-ful the day of___ the moun - tain.

Joe Mattingly
Text and music © 1990, WLP

69 On a Journey Together

1. Walking on cobblestones, tearing my feet to the bones,
   tryin' to make it on my own, wondering where I'm going
   and how I'm gonna get there, sure can't do it all alone.

REFRAIN

On a jour-ney to-geth-er we can fare an-y weath-er, keep-ing Christ the cen-ter of our com-mu-ni-ty. On a jour-ney to-geth-er we can make the world— bet-ter by for-giv-ing and lov-ing, start-ing with you and me.

2. All of the mistakes I made, taking many wrong turns,
   are really lessons that I learned. So ev'ry time I start to stumble,
   I remain humble to God's love and his Word.

3. Trav'ling on this road to Jesus, knowing that vision is the key
   to understand where we've been and where we are and want to be,
   now it starts with you and me.

John Angotti
Text and music © 1998, WLP

REFRAIN

Je - sus, in this great sac - ra - ment, you nour-ish and strength-en our ho - li - ness, that we might walk in the light of one faith, and in one com- mun- ion of love. _____

To Verses

Final

love. _____ That we might walk in the light of one faith, and in one com- mun - ion of love. _____

VERSES

1. Our Lord gave him - self as an un - blem-ished of- f'ring, a
2. When we eat this meal, we re- mem- ber Christ's pas- sion, and
3. We come then to you, to be fed at your ta - ble, that

To Refrain

1. most fit - ting gift for the glo - ry of God. _____
2. share in his pow'r till the end of all time. _____
3. we may all grow in the like - ness of Christ. _____

James V. Marchionda
Text and music © 1995, WLP

71 Only in God

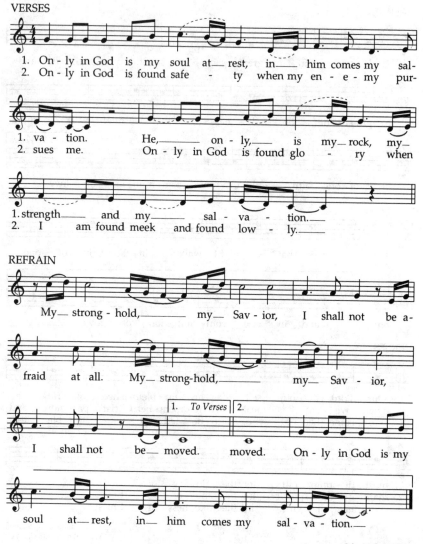

VERSES

1. On - ly in God is my soul at___ rest, in___ him comes my sal-
2. On - ly in God is found safe - ty when my en - e - my pur-

1. va - tion. He,___ on - ly,___ is my___ rock, my
2. sues me. On - ly in God is found glo - ry when

1. strength___ and my___ sal - va - tion.___
2. I am found meek and found low - ly.___

REFRAIN

My___ strong - hold,___ my___ Sav - ior, I shall not be a-

fraid at all. My___ strong-hold,___ my___ Sav - ior,

1. *To Verses* | 2.

I shall not be___ moved. moved. On - ly in God is my

soul at___ rest, in___ him comes my sal - va - tion.___

John Michael Talbot
Text and music © 1980, Birdwing Music/BMG Songs

1. Praise him all you nations. Oh, praise him with your dancing.
   Praise him with the angels, Oh, praise him with singing.
   Come, eat the bread, come and drink the wine.

REFRAIN

2. Glory to the Father, Oh, glory to the Spirit,
   Holy God is with us, sing glory, he is Jesus.
   Come, eat the bread, come and drink the wine.

Ed Bolduc
Text and music © 1992, WLP

73 Our God Reigns

VERSES

1. How love-ly on the moun-tains are the feet of him
2. He had no state - ly form. He had no maj - es - ty
3. It was our sin and guilt that bruised and wound-ed him,
4. Meek as a lamb that's led out to the slaugh-ter-house,
5. Out of the tomb he came with grace and maj - es - ty,

1. who brings good news, good news;
2. that we should be drawn to him.
3. it was our sin brought him down.
4. still as a sheep be - fore its shearer,
5. he is a - live, he is a - live!

1. An-nounc-ing peace, pro-claim-ing news of hap - pi - ness:
2. He was de-spised and we took no ac-count of him;
3. When we like sheep had gone a - stray, our shep-herd came
4. His life ran down up - on the ground like pour-ing rain
5. God loves us so; see here his hands, his feet, his side:

1. our God reigns, our God reigns!
2. yet now he reigns with the Most High!
3. and on his shoul - ders bore our shame!
4. that we might be born a - gain!
5. yes, we know he is a - live!

REFRAIN

Our God reigns, our God reigns,

our God reigns, our God reigns!

Is 52:7; Lk 24:5, 6, 39

Leonard E. Smith, Jr.
Text and music © 1974, 1978, New Jerusalem Music

REFRAIN

Out of the depths I cry__ to you, O Lord._____

1. If you, O Lord, mark our sins,
   O Lord, who can stand?
   But with you is forgiveness
   that you may be revered.

2. I trust in the Lord,
   my soul trusts in God's word.
   My soul waits for the Lord
   more than those who wait for the dawn.

3. For with the Lord is kindness
   and plentiful redemption.
   Our God will redeem Israel
   from all their iniquities.

Mike Hay, 1953–1999
Music © 1993, WLP

75 **Praise God!**

REFRAIN

Cantor

Praise God!_____ Praise him in his ho-ly tem-ple!___

Assembly

Praise God!_____

To Verses

Praise God!_____

To Verses

Praise him in his ho-ly tem-ple!___ Praise God!___

VERSES

Cantor

1. Praise his strength in heav-en! Praise him for the might-y
2. Praise him with the trum-pets! Praise him on the lute_ and
3. Praise the Lord with cym-bals! Play them loud and make a

Assembly

1. things he's done!_____ Praise him, all you peo-ple,
2. on the harp!_____ Praise him in the dance and
3. joy-ful noise!_____ Sing to-geth-er now and

Praise God! Praise God!_____

To Refrain
(Last time to Final Refrain)

1. for the Lord our God is___ great!___
2. praise the Lord with flute and___ drum!___
3. lift your voice un - to the___ Lord!___

To Refrain
(Last time to Final Refrain)

FINAL REFRAIN

Cantor
Praise God!___ Praise him in his ho - ly tem - ple!___

Assembly
Praise God!___

Praise God!___

Praise him in his ho - ly tem - ple! Praise God!___

Praise God!___

Praise God!___

Paul A. Tate
Text and music © 1996, WLP

76 Rain Down

REFRAIN

Cantor/All

Rain down, rain your love on me,— rain— down.

Rain down, rain your love on me.—

Rain down, rain your love on me,— rain— down.

Rain down, rain your love on— me.

VERSE

Cantor

Give me strength,— Lord,— give me the strength to up-

hold your name.— Give me faith,— Lord,—

Give me the faith to up-hold your name.— Let your

love shine a light on my— way. Let your light shine and

show me your way; we are your chil-dren, O God!

Rain your love— on me. Rain your love— on me.

FINAL REFRAIN

Cantor/All

Rain down, rain your love on me, — rain — down.

Rain down, rain your love on me. —

Rain down, rain your love on me, — rain — down.

Rain down, rain your love on me. —

Rain your love — on me. Rain your love — on me.

Rain your love — on me. Rain your love!

Ed Bolduc
Text and music © 1994, WLP

77 Reason To Live

REFRAIN

Cantor/All

I will love the Lord always and for-ev-er. He will be my strength that comes from God a-bove. And I will serve the Lord. He will be my pas-sion. He will be my rea-son to hope, my rea-son to live.

VERSES

Cantor

1. No one who be-lieves shall ev-er thirst. No one who be-lieves shall hun-ger a-gain. All who come to him shall live for-
2. Je-sus, Liv-ing Bread, bring us new life. Je-sus, Lamb of God, bring us new hope. Je-sus, Bread of Life, you make us one

To Refrain

1. ev - er.
2. bod - y.

Ed Bolduc
Text and music © 1993, WLP

REFRAIN   **Search Me, O God** 78

Search me, O God, and know my heart; test me and know my

in - most thoughts; seek in my soul for paths that are wrong, and

lead me, lead me in the ways that are ev - er - last - ing.

1. O Lord, you know me through and through,
   you know my rising, sitting down;
   you discern my thoughts from far away;
   you search me out, you know my soul,
   you know my walking, lying down;
   all my ways, all my ways lie open to you.

2. Before a word is on my tongue,
   you know, O Lord, the whole if it;
   you hem me in from ev'ry side,
   your hand is always laid on me.
   This knowledge is too great for me,
   too wonderful, too high, beyond my reach.

3. Oh, where can I escape your love, where can I flee your presence here?
   If I ascend to heaven, you are there;
   if I sleep in Sheol, you are there.

4. And if I fly on wings of dawn and dwell beyond the farthest seas,
   even there your hand would lead me and guide me;
   your strong right hand would hold me firmly.

5. And if I ask the dark to hide me, light around me be as night,
   even darkness is not dark for you;
   the night becomes as bright as day,
   for they are both the same in your sight.

Paul Inwood
Text and music © 1991, 1992, Paul Inwood, pub. and dist. by WLP

79 Send Forth Your Spirit, O Lord

REFRAIN

Send forth your Spir-it, O Lord,_____ and re-new the face of the earth._____ Send forth your Spir-it, O Lord, and re-new the face of the earth._____

VERSES

Cantor

1. Bless_____ the Lord,_____ O_____ my soul, Lord
2. Lord,_____ my God,_____ great are your works! In
3. All of your crea-tures look_____ to you, to

1. God,_____ how great you are,_____
2. wis-dom you made them all._____
3. give them their food in time._____ You

1. wrapped in a gar-ment of glo-ry and might,_____
2. Rich is the earth_____ and filled with your life._____
3. give with a-bun-dance, they gath-er it up,_____

To Refrain

1. _____ clothed in light as in_____ a robe._____
2. _____ Bless the Lord, O bless,_____ my soul!_____
3. _____ by your hands they have_____ their fill._____

Steven C. Warner
Text and music © 1996, WLP

Set Your Heart on the Higher Gifts

80

REFRAIN

Cantor/All

Set your heart on the high-er gifts,— on the things that come from your Mak-er in heav-en. These three gifts are all that re-main: faith, hope and love, and the great-est is love.

VERSES

Cantor

1. If I speak with the tongues of the liv-ing,
2. And if I un-der-stand ev-'ry mys-t'ry,
3. And if I should re-nounce all my rich-es,

1. and of an-gels, but speak with-out love, I am on-ly
2. hav-ing wis-dom, but think with-out love, had I faith to
3. feed the hun-gry, give o-ver my life; with-out love my

To Refrain

1. brass with-out song, an emp-ty noise on the wind.
2. scat-ter the hills,— I am noth-ing at all.
3. prof-it is loss, my car-ing finds no re-ward.

1 Cor 12:31–13:13

Steven C. Warner
Adapt. text and music © 1992, 1994, WLP

81 Send Us Flowing Water

REFRAIN

Send us flow-ing wa-ter, Lord,__ we shall all re-ceive.

__ Send us flow-ing wa-ter, Lord,__

1.-3. we shall all be-lieve! | Final lieve! Send us flow-ing

wa-ter, Lord!__ We shall all be-lieve.

Joe Mattingly
Text and music © 1988, WLP

82 Shine on Us, Lord

REFRAIN

So shine on us, Lord,__ we're call-ing; send down your light.

__ Please shine on us, Lord,__ we need you to save us, Lord,

__ and bring us home__ to your ev-er-last-ing light.__

VERSES

1. We call the Lord by name, for God a-lone can
2. O bless the Lord, my soul,__ for God a-lone is

1. save us.—
2. ho - ly.—

1. Cry out to God with joy— and sing his
2. Send down your spir - it, Lord, and all your

To Refrain

1. glo - ri - ous name to all— the— earth. O— Lord!
2. peo - ple will clap their hands and— sing. O— Lord!

Joe Mattingly
Text and music © 1985, Joe Mattingly

Show Us the Way 83

1. Show us the way to bring light to the darkness
   covering all the earth!
   Show us the way to embrace one another,
   opening hearts for rebirth!

REFRAIN

Show us the way— as we go forth in love.—

Show us the way— as we go forth in peace.—

Show us the way— as we go forth to serve.—

Lead us, O Lord!— Show— us the way!—

2. Show us the way to be seekers of freedom,
   breaking the chains of our fear.
   Show us the way to speak peace to all people,
   strengthening all those who hear.

3. Show us the way; give us strength for the journey,
   letting your light lead the way.
   Show us the way; bring us home to your kingdom.
   Lifting our voices we pray:

Deanna Light and Paul A. Tate
Text and music © 1997, WLP

Song of Judith

REFRAIN
Cantor/Assembly

Sing to God with the tam - bour - ine, sing with cym - bals in praise of the Lord! Raise a can - ti - cle!

Last time to Coda ⊕

To Verses

Ring out the name of God!_____

⊕ CODA

God!_____ Raise a can - ti - cle! Ring out the name_____ of God!_____

VERSES
Cantor

1. Sing to God with the tam - bour and drum, with
2. I will sing a new song to my God:
3. For you spoke and it all came to be, the
4. Should the moun - tains be tossed from their base, to

1. cym - bals in hon - or of God._____
2. Lord, you are glo - ri - ous and great._____
3. force of your breath built it up._____ Your
4. mix with the waves of the sea,_____ if the

1. Sing to the Lord! Raise up a psalm! Re -
2. Source of our strength! Mar - v'lous in might, may
3. Spir - it pre - vailed! Called us as one, to
4. stones were to melt like wax in your sight, your

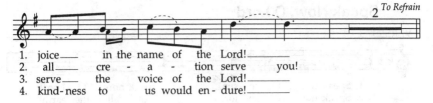

2 *To Refrain*

1. joice___ in the name of the Lord!___
2. all___ cre - a - tion serve you!
3. serve___ the voice of the Lord!___
4. kind-ness to us would en - dure!___

Jdt 16:1–2, 13–15
Adapt. by S.C.W.

Steven C. Warner
Text and music © 1993, WLP

Sometimes by Step 85

REFRAIN

O God, you are my___ God, and I will ev- er praise you.

O God, you are my___ God, and I will ev- er praise you.

I will seek you in the morn - ing,___ and I will

learn to walk in your___ ways,___ and step by step you lead

___ me,___ and I will fol-low you all of my___ days.

1. Sometimes the night was beautiful, sometimes the sky was so far away,
   sometimes it seemed to steep so close
   you could touch it but your heart would break,
   sometimes the morning came too soon, sometimes the day could be so hot,
   there was so much work left to do, but so much you've already done. Oh,

2. Sometimes I think of Abraham, how one star he saw had been lit for me.
   He was a stranger in this land, and I am that no less than he,
   and on this road to righteousness sometimes
   the climb can be so steep I may falter in my steps
   but never beyond your reach. Oh,

Rich Mullins & Beaker
Text and music © 1992, Edward Grant, Inc./Kid Brothers of St. Francis Publishing

86 Speak Now, O Lord

VERSES

1. Speak now, O Je-sus,__ speak now, O Lord!
2. Speak now, O Sav-ior__ of all the earth!
3. Speak now, O prom-ise!__ God's word re-vealed!
4. Speak now, O lov-er__ of all the world!

1. We come to lis-ten,__ to hear your word.
2. We come to praise you;__ to bless your name.
3. We bow be-fore you,__ we call you Lord!
4. We stand be-fore you,__ to live your word!

1. We come as serv-ants, to do your will.
2. We are the cap-tives, we are the lame.
3. We are the suf-f'ring, for-got-ten ones.
4. We are the hun-gry,__ we are the cold.

REFRAIN

We are your hands and feet! Speak now, speak now!

To Verses | *Final*

Speak now, O Lord._____ Lord. We are your

hands and feet! Speak now, speak now! Speak now, O Lord.

Joe Mattingly
Text and music © 1994, WLP

Strength for the Journey

REFRAIN

I will be,—— I will be,—— I will be

strength for the jour - ney. I will be,—— I will be,—

— I will be strength for the jour - ney.—

VERSES

1. There is a road— meant for you to trav - el.——
2. There is a cross— meant for you to car - ry.——
3. How man-y times have you doubt-ed my— Word?

1. Nar - row and steep is—— the shep-herd's way,— and
2. There is a cross meant for you a - lone, and
3. How man - y times must I call your name? And

1. as you say, "Yes," — let-ting me guide you,—
2. as you bow down in hum-ble sur - ren - der,—
3. as you say, "Yes," — let-ting me love you,—

To Refrain

1.–3. I will be strength— for the jour - ney.——

Michael John Poirier
Text and music © 1988, Michael John Poirier

88 The Face of God

1. I believe in my Lord Jesus, Son of God and Son of man,
   who died and rose for the sake of all. He is the Lamb. Oh.
   I believe that there's a Spirit, a gift to every child of God,
   so as we stumble to make our way, it leads us on. Oh.

REFRAIN

And I be-lieve in God, God of love and God of mer - cy. I be-lieve that I have seen the face of God in the land of the liv-ing.

2. I believe that there's a mercy flowing from the hand of God, my God,
   to wash me clean from the stain of sin. His love goes on. Oh.
   I believe that we are people born to live a life for God.
   And if we follow the shepherd's way, then life goes on. Oh.

Ed Bolduc
Text and music © 1998, WLP

89 The Love of God

REFRAIN

Cantor/All

What can sep - a - rate us from the love of God? Nei-ther hun - ger nor dan - ger, pov - er - ty or death! No, noth-ing sep - a - rates us from the love of God which is ours through Christ Je - sus, the Lord!

To Verses
Cantor

1. If
4. Of

VERSES 1–3

Cantor

1. God is for____ us, who can be a-gainst us?
2. Who can stand as judge? Who will judge the right-eous?
3. Who shall cri-ti-cize? Who will count or meas-ure?

To Refrain

1. Cer-tain-ly____ not God, who has giv-en us his Son!
2. Yes, it is____ our God, who has freed us through his Son!
3. Cer-tain-ly____ not God, who has called us each his own!

VERSE 4

Cantor

4. this much I am sure: noth-ing can di-vide____ us!

4. We have won the bat - tle, u - nit-ed in the Lord!____

FINAL REFRAIN

Cantor/All

What can sep-a-rate____ us from the love of God? Nei-ther

hun-ger nor dan-ger, pov-er-ty____ or death! No,

noth-ing sep-a-rates____ us from the love of God which is

ours through Christ Je-sus, the____ Lord! Which is

ours through Christ Je-sus, the____ Lord!

Based on Rom 8:31–39

Paul A. Tate
Text and music © 1997, WLP

90 The Lord Is Kind and Merciful

REFRAIN

The Lord is kind and mer - ci - ful. *Cantor simile*

The Lord is kind and mer - ci - ful._____

The Lord is kind and mer - ci - ful._____

slow to an - ger, rich__ in com-pas-sion.

The Lord is kind and mer - ci - ful._____

1. My soul, give thanks to the Lord,
   all my being, bless his holy name.
   My soul, give thanks to the Lord
   and never forget all his blessings.

2. It is he who forgives all your guilt,
   who heals every one of your ills,
   who redeems your life from the grave,
   who crowns you with love and compassion.

3. His wrath will come to an end;
   he will not be angry for ever.
   For as the heavens are high above the earth
   so strong is his love for those who fear him.

Text (ref.) © 1969, 1981, ICEL
Text (vss.) © 1963, Ladies of the Grail (England). GIA, exclusive agent

Ed Bolduc
Music © 1998, WLP

Our Fa - ther,—— who art in heav - en,—— hal - low - ed

be thy name;—— thy king-dom come,—— thy will be

done—— on earth as it is in heav - en. Give us this

day—— our dai - ly bread;—— and for - give us our

tres - pass - es—— as we for - give those—— who tres-pass a -

gainst us.—— And lead us—— not in-to temp - ta - tion,——

— but de - liv - er us from e - vil.——

Priest: Deliver us, Lord, from every evil,...

For the king - dom, the pow'r, and the glo - ry——

— are yours, both now and for - ev - er.——

From—— now un - til the end of time.——

The Embolism from the English translation of the *Roman Missal* © 1973, ICEL

Steven C. Warner
Music © 1980, 1993, WLP

The Stranger and the Nets

1.–3. There will be days___ when your nets will come___ back

1. emp - ty, ___ Cast in - to___ the sea of
2. emp - ty, ___ And guilt will leave you stum - bling
3. emp - ty, Tho' you've fought a - gainst the tide's re -

1. bro - ken dreams.___ Let your eyes seek out___ the
2. with the damned.___ ___ Call his name, the
3. lent - less pull.___ On - ly rec - og - nize the

1.–3. stran - ger on___ the sea - shore.___

1.–3. Be- lieve in him, be- lieve in him, be -

13

1. lieve in him, he is more than what he seems!
2. lieve, and help him___ feed the hun - gry lambs.
3. lieve in him, and your nets will come back full.

Rory Cooney and Claire Cooney
Text and music © 1998, WLP

REFRAIN

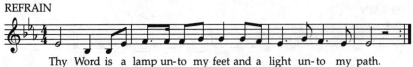

Thy Word is a lamp un-to my feet and a light un-to my path.

VERSES

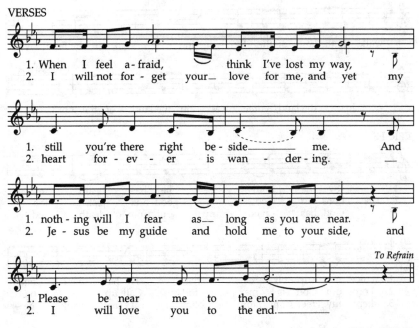

1. When I feel a-fraid, think I've lost my way,
2. I will not for-get your love for me, and yet my

1. still you're there right be-side me. And
2. heart for-ev-er is wan - der-ing.

1. noth - ing will I fear as long as you are near.
2. Je - sus be my guide and hold me to your side, and

To Refrain

1. Please be near me to the end.
2. I will love you to the end.

Amy Grant and Michael W. Smith
Text and music © 1984, Meadowgreen Music/Word Music, Inc.

94 Walk in the Land

REFRAIN

Walk in the land, walk in the land, come walk in the land of the liv - ing. Walk in the land, walk — in — the land, come walk in the land of the Lord.

(⌢) *Last time*

VERSES

1. I love the Lord for he has heard my
2. The Lord our God is good and just, the
3. — God has saved my soul from death and

1. voice in — sup - pli - ca - tion! He has bent his
2. Lord our God is mer - ci - ful! Call up - on — the
3. kept my feet from stum - bling! I shall walk be -

1. ear to me — the day I called his
2. name of God, and God will save your
3. fore the Lord, — walk be - fore the

To Refrain

1. name! — His name! I will
2. life! — Your life! I will
3. Lord! — The Lord! I will

Joe Mattingly
Text and music © 1994, WLP

REFRAIN

Cantor — *All*

1. Wa - ters of life, Wa - ters of life,
2. Wa - ters of life, Wa - ters of life,

Cantor — *All*

1. Cre - at - ing life, Cre - at - ing life,
2. Spir - it of God, Spir - it of God,

Cantor — *All*

1. Bap - tized in faith, Bap - tized in faith,
2. Called as your own, Called as your own,

Cantor — *All*

1. Sealed with your love, Sealed with your love.
2. Light for our lives, Light for our lives.

1. Cleansed from all sin, baptized you are reborn,
   clothed in Christ, anointed priest and prophet, king.
   Welcomed in love, family of faith joined as one,
   we share God's everlasting life.

2. Word of God, present from all time,
   the light that darkness cannot overcome.
   Walk in light now called to be God's own, fire of love,
   flame of faith kept deep within your heart.

3. Blessed be God who's chosen you in Christ,
   work of art, created as the Father's own.
   Cleansed in this stream where life itself unites,
   we share one faith, one family in the Lord.

Laura Kutscher
Text and music © 1992, WLP

96 We Are Faithful

VERSES

1. A rain-bow is a sign of the love of the Lord.
2. The cross is a sign of the pain of our Lord.
3. Chil - dren of God, be a sign to each oth -

1. A rain-bow is a sign of his love.
2. The cross is a sign of his love.
3. - er. You are a sign of his love.

1. We are a sign of his love to the Fa - ther,
2. Sin swept a - way through the death of a Sav - ior.
3. Faith of a child that is shown to the Fa - ther.

1. found in the bread and the wine.
2. Life through the bread and the wine.
3. Faith in the bread and the wine.

REFRAIN

We are faith-ful, Lord, un-to you. We re - mem-ber,

Lord, we re - new. You are the Fa - ther.

We live for you, O Lord.

Ed Bolduc and R.S. Raus

Ed Bolduc
Text and music © 1993, WLP

REFRAIN

We are the hope! We are the fu - ture! Cho - sen by God, com-pelled by the Word! Called to walk in the foot-steps of Je - sus! Build - ing the king - dom, we are the hope!

VERSES

Cantor — *All*

1. For all the proph - ets who go un - heard,
2. For all the chil - dren who have no voice, we are the hope,
3. For ev - 'ry race and for ev - 'ry kind,

Cantor — *All*

1. and all who seek to o - bey your Word,
2. and all the un - born who have no choice, we are the hope!
3. till ev - 'ry per - son is col - or - blind,

Cantor — *All*

1. For all who suf - fer the pain of war,
2. For all the peo - ple who live in fear, we are the hope,
3. To those im - pris - oned by sin and greed,

Cantor — *All* — *To Refrain*

1. and all who re - build, re - new, re - store,
2. and all who doubt that our God is near, we are the hope!
3. and all who judge by be - lief or creed,

Paul A. Tate
Text and music © 1998, WLP

98 We Are One Body

REFRAIN

We are one bod - y,___ one bod - y in Christ;___ and we
do not stand a - lone. We are one bod -
- y___ one bod - y in Christ;___ and he
came that we might have life.___ *(1.–6.)* *To Verses*

Final
— He came that we might have life.

VERSES 1, 2, 4, 5

1. When you eat my bod - y and you drink my
2. Can you hear them cry - ing, can you feel their
4. I have come, your Sav - ior, that you might have
5. At the name of Je - sus ev - 'ry knee shall

1. blood, I will live in you___ and you will live in my
2. pain? Will you feed my hun - gry, will you help___ my
4. life, through the tears and sor - row, through the toils___ and
5. bend; Je - sus is the Lord___ and he will come___ a -

1. love. When you eat my bod - y and you drink my
2. lame? See the un - born ba - by, the for - got - ten
4. strife. Lis - ten when I call___ you, for I know your
5. gain. At the name of Je - sus ev - 'ry knee shall

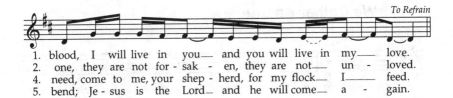

1. blood, I will live in you— and you will live in my— love.
2. one, they are not for - sak - en, they are not— un - loved.
4. need, come to me, your shep - herd, for my flock— I— feed.
5. bend; Je - sus is the Lord— and he will come— a - gain.

3. I am the Way, the Truth, the Life,
   I am the Final Sacrifice,
   I am the Way, the Truth, the Life,
   he who believes in me will have eternal life.

6. On the rock of Peter, see my Church I build.
   Come receive my spirit, with my gifts be filled.
   For you are my body, you're my hands and feet.
   Speak my word of life to everyone you meet.

Dana Scallon
Text and music © 1993, Heartbeat Music

We Gather Here 99

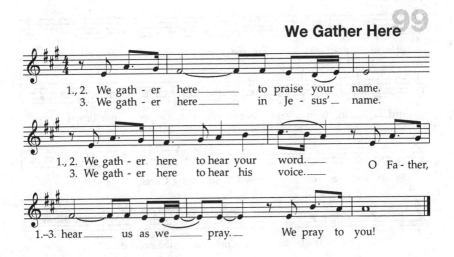

1., 2. We gath - er here_____ to praise your name.
3. We gath - er here_____ in Je - sus'_ name.

1., 2. We gath - er here to hear your word.__ O Fa - ther,
3. We gath - er here to hear his voice.__

1.–3. hear_____ us as we_____ pray. — We pray to you!

1. "When you call to me I will answer you.
   I'll rescue you and give you honor.
   Long life I will give you and bless you."
   Lord, hear us now. Lord, hear us now.

Ed Bolduc
Text and music © 1993, WLP

100 We Gather As One

VERSE 1

Gath-ered at ta - ble to join in the feast,___ u - nit - ed in
spir - it the great - est, the least. Lift - ing our voic - es, we
gath - er as one, called to bring Christ to the world.___
— We are called to bring Christ to the world!

VERSE 2

Voice of the Spir - it, our gos - pel to share,___ u - nit - ed in
word,___ in faith and in prayer. O - pen our hearts, we
lis - ten as one, called to bring Christ to the world.___
— We are called to bring Christ to the world!

VERSE 3

Har - vest of plen - ty, God's life - giv-ing bread,___ u -
nit - ed with Je - sus in birth and in death. Food for the

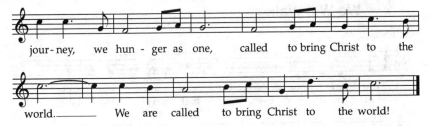

jour-ney, we hun - ger as one, called to bring Christ to the

world.___ We are called to bring Christ to the world!

Carol Dinise and Cathryn Howard
Text and music © 1998, WLP

We Receive Power 101

We re - ceive pow - er*, re - ceive pow - er, re -

ceive the pow-er of God, when the Ho - ly Spir - it

comes_ to us. We re - ceive the pow-er of God.

Oh,___ come, Ho - ly Spir - it, come___ to us.

Come, Ho - ly Spir - it, come. Come and

fill us with the pow - er,___ fill us with the pow - er,___

2

fill us with the pow - er of God.

James V. Marchionda
Text and music © 1995, WLP

*Additional verses: 2. wisdom, 3. courage, 4. mercy, 5. glory, 6. freedom, 7. blessing, 8. kindness

102 We Will Walk

VERSES

1. You are our strength. You are our guide.
2. Lift up your eyes, high o'er the hills.

1. We look to you and are saved!_____
2. See, your help comes from the Lord._____

1. Je - sus, our Lord, Je - sus, our light,
2. Mer - cy__ and love live with - in__ you.

1. come, show your peo - ple__ new life!
2. Come, show your peo - ple__ new life!

REFRAIN

And we will walk with the Fa - ther,__ and we will

run to the Son__ far a - way from all the

e - vil that dwells in our world._____ And we will

turn to each oth - er,__ and we will live in the Lord

__ for all e - ter - ni - ty!_____

Ed Bolduc
Text and music © 1993, WLP

1. Do you believe in God, the Father, the Almighty,
   maker of heaven and earth?

REFRAIN

Yes, we— be-lieve,— we do, Lord! Yes, we— be-lieve,— — we do, Lord! Yes, we— be-lieve,— we do, Lord!—

2. Do you believe in Jesus, God's only Son, our Lord,
   who was born of the Virgin Mary, was crucified under Pontius Pilate,
   suffered and died, and was buried?

3. Do you believe that on the third day he rose from the dead,
   and is now seated at the Father's right hand?

4. Do you believe in the Holy Spirit? (Yes, we believe, we do, Lord!)
   In the Lord, the giver of all life? (Yes, we believe...)
   With the Father and Son, he is worshiped and glorified.
   (Yes, we believe...)
   He has spoken to us through the Prophets. (Yes, we believe...)
   Do you believe in the holy catholic Church, (Yes, we believe...)
   one baptism for the forgiveness of all sin? (Yes, we believe...)
   Do you believe that the dead shall rise,
   and in life of the world to come? Amen!

Paul A. Tate
Music © 1996, WLP

104 You

What shall I call you? How shall I name you?

How can I show you my shad-ows?____

How will you hear me____ if I have nev-er named you, and a-

shamed, have con-demned you to shad-ows?____

1. You, I know you in thunder and lightning.
   You, you strike my heart to the core.
   I cannot ignore your call, sparkling in the dawn.

2. You, you are unmeasured in splendor.
   You, you move in earthquake and fire,
   the fierceness of desire, shuddering in the dawn.

3. You, dissolving the webs of illusion,
   You, you sing and boundaries shake,
   the music in me wakes, surprising as the dawn.

4. You, you are my guardian invisible.
   You, you are the night wind and moon,
   my stars, my earth, my sun, you're dancing in the dawn.

Rory Cooney and Claire Cooney
Text and music © 1998, WLP

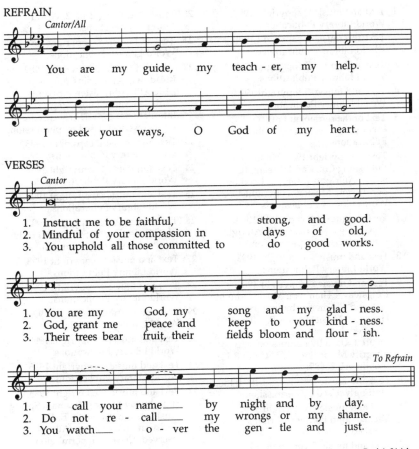

REFRAIN

Cantor/All

You are my guide, my teach-er, my help.

I seek your ways, O God of my heart.

VERSES

Cantor

1. Instruct me to be faithful, strong, and good.
2. Mindful of your compassion in days of old,
3. You uphold all those committed to do good works.

1. You are my God, my song and my glad-ness.
2. God, grant me peace and keep to your kind-ness.
3. Their trees bear fruit, their fields bloom and flour-ish.

To Refrain

1. I call your name___ by night and by day.
2. Do not re-call___ my wrongs or my shame.
3. You watch___ o-ver the gen-tle and just.

Paul A. Lisicky
Text and music © 1995, WLP

106 Acknowledgments

1 Text and music © copyright 1993, World Library Publications.

2 Text and music © copyright 1998, World Library Publications.

3 Text and music © copyright 1998 World Library Publications.

4 Text and music © copyright 1993, World Library Publications.

5 Text of the refrain and music © copyright 1998, World Library Publications.

6 Text © copyright 1989, Hope Publishing Co., Carol Stream, IL 60188. All rights reserved. Used by permission. Music © copyright 1993, World Library Publications.

7 Text and music © copyright 1988, BMG Songs, Inc. (ASCAP). All rights reserved. Used by permission.

8 Text and music © copyright 1993, World Library Publications.

9 Text and music © copyright 1982, Kingsway's Thankyou Music (adm in N, S and C America by Integrity's Hosanna! Music)/ASCAP. All rights reserved. International copyright secured. Used by permission. c/o Integrity Music, Inc., 1000 Cody Rd., Mobile, AL 36685.

10 Text and music © copyright 1994, Joe Mattingly. Used by permission.

11 Text and music © copyright 1992, Michael John Poirier. All rights reserved.

12 Text and music © copyright 1995, World Library Publications.

13 Text and music © copyright 1996, World Library Publications.

14 Arrangement © copyright 1989, World Library Publications. None for pew

15 Text and music © copyright 1993, World Library Publications.

16 Text and music © copyright 1993, Joe Mattingly. Used by permission.

17 Text and music © copyright 1997, World Library Publications.

18 Text and music © copyright 1980, Birdwing Music (ASCAP)/BMG Songs (CL)(ASCAP). Administered by EMI Christian Music Group. All rights reserved. Used with permission.

19 Text and music © copyright 1997, World Library Publications.

20 Music © copyright 1992, World Library Publications.

21 Text and music © copyright 1994, World Library Publications.

22 Text and music © copyright 1982, Meadowgreen Music Company (ASCAP). Administered by EMI Christian Music Publishing. International copyright secured. All rights reserved. Used by permission.

23 Text and music © copyright 1998, World Library Publications.

24 Text and music © copyright 1998, World Library Publications.

25 Text and music © copyright 1997, World Library Publications.

26 Text and music © copyright 1993, BMG Songs, Inc. (ASCAP). All rights reserved. Used by permission.

27 Text and music © copyright 1998, World Library Publications.

28 Text and music © copyright 1998, World Library Publications.

29 Text and music © copyright 1995, World Library Publications.

30 Text and music © copyright 1998, World Library Publications.

31 Text and music © copyright 1995, World Library Publications.

32 Text and music © copyright 1985, Straightway Music/Mountain Spring Music. Administered by EMI Christian Music Group. All rights reserved. Used with permission.

33 Text of the refrain from the *Lectionary for Mass*, © copyright 1969, 1981, International Committee on English in the Liturgy, Inc. (ICEL). All rights reserved. Text of the verses and music © copyright 1993, 1997, World Library Publications.

34 Text and music © copyright 1992, World Library Publications.

35 Text and music © copyright 1998, World Library Publications.

36 Text and music © copyright 1993, World Library Publications.

37 Text and music © copyright 1980, Birdwing Music (ASCAP)/BMG Songs (CL)(ASCAP). Administered by EMI Christian Music Group. All rights reserved. Used with permission.

38 Text and music © copyright 1998, World Library Publications.

108 Topical Index

Many of the songs in *Voices As One* are also available on recordings and in other editions from World Library Publications. Order items below through WLP Customer Service, 3825 N. Willow Rd., Schiller Park, IL 60176 by telephone at 1 800 566-6150 by FAX at 1 888 WLP-FAX1 or e-mail to wlpcs@jspaluch.com.

1 All Will Be Well
recordings:
Of Holy Women,
cassette 7326, CD 7328
The Seven Signs,
cassette 7236, CD 7238
Your Morn Shall Rise, CD 3370
songbook:
Your Morn Shall Rise, 3372
octavo: 7206

2 Alleluia! Your Word, O Lord
recording:
The Face of God,
cassette 7442, CD 7444
octavo: 7350

3 Answer When I Call
recording:
Let All Creation Sing,
cassette 7468, CD 7470
songbooks:
Gathered As One, 7457
Let All Creation Sing, 7473
octavo: 7483

4 Answer Me
recordings:
Heaven and Earth,
cassette 7406, CD 7408
We Are Faithful,
cassette 7420, CD 7422
songbooks:
Collection, Liturgical Music, 7400
We Are Faithful, 7441
octavo: 7448

5 At the Name of Jesus
recording:
The Face of God,
cassette 7442, CD 7444
octavo: 7351

6 At the Table of the World
recording:
Veni, Creator Spiritus,
cassette 2640, CD 2630
octavo: 2612

8 Be Holy
recording:
I Believe, cassette 7402
songbook:
Collection, Liturgical Music, 7400

10 Be with Me, Lord
recording:
Be with Me, Lord,
cassette 3612
songbook:
Be with Me, Lord, 3610
octavo: 3678

11 Bread of Life
recording:
Ocean of Mercy,
cassette 2671, CD 2676
songbook:
Michael John Poirier Songbook, 2675

12 Build a Family
recording:
Heaven and Earth,
cassette 7406, CD 7408

13 By the Waters of Babylon
recording:
Cornerstone,
cassette 2338, CD 2340
Let All Creation Sing,
cassette 7468, CD 7470
songbooks:
Gathered As One, 7457
Let All Creation Sing, 7473
octavo: 7451

14 Christ, Be Near at Either Hand
recording:
Mass on the Feast of St. Patrick,
cassette 7318
Crossroads of Praise,
cassette 7256, CD 7258
octavo: 7200

15 Come, Christians, Unite
recording:
We Are Faithful,
cassette 7420, CD 7422
songbooks:
Collection, Liturgical Music, 7400
We Are Faithful, 7441
octavo: 7417

16 Come Home
recording:
Every Age, cassette 3662
songbook:
Every Age, 3660
octavo: 3673

43 I Turn to You
recording:
Walk in the Land,
cassette 3614, CD 3616
songbook:
Walk in the Land, 3618
octavo: 3679

44 I Will Praise Your Name
recording:
The Face of God,
cassette 7442, CD 7444
octavo: 7438

45 If Today You Hear the Voice of God
recording:
The Face of God,
cassette 7442, CD 7444
octavo: 7352

46 In Remembrance of You
recording:
Gathered As One,
cassette 7460, CD 7462
songbook:
Gathered As One, 7457

47 In the Arms of the Shepherd
recording:
Road to Emmaus,
cassette 2352, CD 2354
Your Morn Shall Rise, CD 3370
songbook:
Your Morn Shall Rise, 3372
octavo: 5657

48 In the Light
recording:
Hello Lord,
cassette 2670, CD 2677
songbook:
Michael John Poirier Songbook, 2675

49 In You, O Lord
recording:
The Face of God,
cassette 7442, CD 7444
octavo: 7439

50 Journey for Home
recording:
The Face of God,
cassette 7442, CD 7444
octavo: 7437

51 Let All Creation Sing Alleluia
recording:
Let All Creation Sing,
cassette 7468, CD 7470
songbook:
Let All Creation Sing, 7473
octavo: 7491

52 Lay Down That Spirit
recording:
Walk in the Land,
cassette 3614, CD 3616
songbook:
Walk in the Land, 3618
octavo: 3674

54 Let Us Sing
recording:
The Face of God,
cassette 7442, CD 7444
octavo: 7353

55 Live In Me
recording:
The Face of God,
cassette 7442, CD 7444
octavo: 7354

56 Lift Your Hearts to the Holy One
recording:
Let All Creation Sing,
cassette 7468, CD 7470
songbooks:
Gathered As One, 7457
Let All Creation Sing, 7473

57 Look to the One
recordings:
I Believe, cassette 7402
We Are Faithful,
cassette 7420, CD 7422
songbooks:
Collection, Liturgical Music, 7400
We Are Faithful, 7441
octavo: 7418

58 Lord, You Are Good
recording:
We Are Faithful,
cassette 7420, CD 7422
songbooks:
Collection, Liturgical Music, 7400
We Are Faithful, 7441
octavo: 7427

59 Lord, Bless Your People
recording:
Candled Seasons,
cassette 7310, CD 7312
octavo: 6205

61 Lord, You Have the Words
recording:
The Face of God,
cassette 7442, CD 7444
octavo: 7355

62 Lord, You Have the Words
of Everlasting Life
octavo: 8543